TRACING YOUR BRITISH INDIAN ANCESTORS

FAMILY HISTORY FROM PEN & SWORD

TRACING YOUR BRITISH INDIAN ANCESTORS

A Guide for Family Historians

Emma Jolly

Pen & Sword
FAMILY HISTORY

First published in Great Britain in 2012 by
PEN & SWORD FAMILY HISTORY
An imprint of
Pen & Sword Books Ltd
47 Church Street
Barnsley
South Yorkshire
S70 2AS

ISBN 978-1-84884-573-2

A CIP catalogue record for this book is available from the British Library.

Typeset by Concept, Huddersfield, West Yorkshire.
Printed and bound in England by CPI Group (UK) Ltd, Croydon, CR0 4YY.

Pen & Sword Books Ltd incorporates the imprints of
Pen & Sword Aviation, Pen & Sword Family History, Pen & Sword Maritime,
Pen & Sword Military, Pen & Sword Discovery, Wharncliffe Local History,
Wharncliffe True Crime, Wharncliffe Transport, Pen & Sword Select,
Pen & Sword Military Classics, Leo Cooper, The Praetorian Press,
Remember When, Seaforth Publishing and Frontline Publishing.

For a complete list of Pen & Sword titles please contact
PEN & SWORD BOOKS LIMITED
47 Church Street, Barnsley, South Yorkshire, S70 2AS, England
E-mail: enquiries@pen-and-sword.co.uk
Website: www.pen-and-sword.co.uk

CONTENTS

ACKNOWLEDGEMENTS

This book would never have existed without the idea from Simon Fowler and his persistence in ensuring it became reality. I am very grateful to him for asking me to write it. At Pen & Sword, I am grateful to Rupert Harding for editorial support and patiently answering scores of emails; and to Pamela Covey for her editing.

Much of my research has taken place in the Asian and African Studies Reading Room at the British Library. All staff members there continue to be invaluable in their assistance, and the enquiries team, particularly, has been consistently helpful and efficient.

I should also like to acknowledge my friends and fellow genealogists, many of whom have been very supportive throughout the preparations for this book. Justine Taylor generously gave me the benefit of her extensive military history and editing expertise. Chris Paton has shown continuous support on his blog http://britishgenes.blogspot.com and kindly taken time to read and comment on several chapters.

In addition, I continue to be inspired by the individuals and families that I research, and I am fortunate that a number of clients were happy for me to reproduce parts of their family histories. I extend sincere thanks to Guy Dixon of Jersey, John Stephens, and Mike Rainey.

As a member of the wonderful FIBIS family history society, I have been greatly assisted by fellow members giving general words of encouragement, sharing family or personal memories, and allowing me to use material in this book. Special thanks go to FIBIS member and volunteer, Noel Gunther; FIBIS Webmaster, Valmay Young; FIBIS Chairman, Peter Bailey; FIBIS Trustee, Elaine MacGregor; and to Valmay's grandmother, Betty Gascoyne, for sharing her photographs and memories.

I receive almost daily support from friends and followers on Twitter. Warm thanks are due, especially, to Jane Fleming, Matthew Ward, genetic genealogist Debbie Kennett, military historian Paul Reed, and The Army Children Archive (www.archhistory.co.uk) for allowing their images and family memories to be included here. Also thanks to railway historian David Turner of http://turniprail.blogspot.com for his reading and invaluable advice.

I am grateful to Hugh Purcell who kindly allowed me to quote from his excellent book *After the Raj: The Last Stayers-On and the Legacy of British India.*

Thanks also to my parents, Barry and Alethea Jolly, who manfully read each early draft and gave valuable advice. And my final and biggest thanks go to my husband, Simon Causer and our children, Jacob and Oscar, for providing much-needed distraction and fun.

PREFACE

This book is aimed at anyone who is tracing British ancestors who were born, lived or worked in the Indian region between 1600 and the late twentieth century. While the official period known as British India is that of the *Raj*, British involvement in India largely dates from the time of the East India Company (later the British East India Company).

In 1700, the population of India was twenty times that of Britain. Despite this, British dominance in India grew to such an extent that, eventually, more than 250 million Indians were being governed by 900 British civil servants with the support of 70,000 British soldiers.[1] Britain became a global superpower in a way that would never have been possible without India, which was later described by Prime Minister Disraeli as 'the brightest jewel of the crown' in the British Empire. Yet there had been no grand plan for this world dominance. Instead, the Empire evolved gradually from very simple beginnings.

Today the term 'British Indian' or 'British-Indian' is used to describe British citizens who are ethnically Indian. Similar considerations apply to the citizens of modern-day Pakistan, Bangladesh and Sri Lanka. In this book, however, the term is used to refer to the British who lived and worked in India during the time of British control. This may include Britons of Indian descent and those with ancestors from elsewhere in Europe and Asia.

The reason for this usage is that other terms are insufficient in their implication. 'British *Raj* ancestors' would limit only to those who lived between 1858 and 1947. And the term 'Anglo-Indian' (and its earlier form, 'Indo-British') has been used in different ways in different periods by different authors.

One example of this may be found in *White Mughals* by William Dalrymple, who refers to the children of English fathers and Indian women in the eighteenth century as 'Anglo-Indian children'.[2] He also writes of 'the burgeoning mixed-blood Anglo-Indian community' of the 1780s and of Cornwallis's legislation that banned 'Anglo-Indian children of British soldiers from entering the East India Company's army between 1786 and 1795'.[3] Most dictionaries today use Anglo-Indian in this way, describing people with mixed British and Indian ancestry. Usually, the male side was British and the female side Indian, although Anglo-Indians who were born in Britain usually had Indian fathers and British mothers.

This term was used to describe people of mixed descent in the 1911 census of India and today, Article 366(2) of the Indian Constitution provides this definition:

> An Anglo-Indian means a person whose Father or any of whose other male progenitors in the male line is or was of European descent, but who is domiciled within the territory of India and is or was born within such territory of parents habitually resident therein and not established there for temporary purposes only.

In the past the term was also used to describe Britons who were born and raised in India (see, for example, the works of Rudyard Kipling). People of mixed descent were known as 'Eurasians' but the term was later used more widely to encompass anyone of mixed European and Asian descent. The Anglo-Indian community came to include those with Portuguese, British, Indian and other European ancestry. Although Anglo-Indians were often segregated and discriminated against, they made an essential contribution to British India and are found in most British Indian records. Therefore, this book covers records relevant to Britons, Europeans and Anglo-Indians in India.

Colonial historians have written at length about negative aspects of British India. However, through the lens of family history, British India can be viewed from an impartial perspective. Throughout the centuries of British rule in India, the country saw every kind of British Indian: from the immensely wealthy and powerful, to the downtrodden and poverty-stricken; from the kind-hearted and generous, to the cruel and greedy; from the technically innovative, to the completely uneducated. It would be unhelpful to attempt to place your own British Indian ancestors in narrow categories. As you will find through your research, each British Indian was unique and made an individual contribution to his or her own world, the Empire, and India today.

Hopefully this book will help you to discover just what that individual contribution was, and how your unique British Indian ancestor affected the world in which he or she lived.

Notes
1. Niall Ferguson, *Empire*.
2. William Dalrymple, *White Mughals*, p.49.
3. Ibid., p.144.

GLOSSARY

A2A	Access to Archives website
AAS	Asian and African Studies, formerly the Asia Pacific and African studies APAC, British Library, London
ayah	nanny or nurse caring for children
bagh	garden or park
bibi	female companion
BL	British Library
box-wallah	a derogatory term for a European businessman
Brahmin	the highest caste/priests and academics
bungalow	country house
cantonment	military area or station
covenanted	those who entered into a covenant with the EIC or Secretary of State for India to become a regular member of the Indian Civil Service
diwani	the rule of an Indian princely state; those who rule are *Dewan*s
EIC	East India Company
Factor	an agent for the factories
Factory	warehouse
FIBIS	Families in British India Society
grass widow	wife at hill station while husband works in the plains
hill stations	towns founded by the British Indians in the hills; cooler than the plains
ICS	Indian Civil Service
INA	Indian National Army
IOR	India Office Records
jagir	a small territory on which tenants pay rent. *Jagirs* were granted by an Indian ruler to military leaders in recognition of service done
jungle-wallah	forest officer
memsahib	British married woman in India
Mofussil	referred to rural areas bordering the Presidency capitals of Bombay, Calcutta and Madras; later the term was used sometimes derogatorily for other rural areas

mufti	civilian clothes
nabob	deputy; used to mean governor
nawab	Provincial governor of the Mughal Empire
NMM	National Maritime Museum
Presidency	administrative area
pukka	proper
raj	rule
Rajahs	Indian aristocracy
RIEC	Royal Indian Engineering College, Cooper's Hill
sahib	Sir, particularly when addressing a European
sepoy	Indian soldier in the service of the British
SOAS	School of Oriental and Asian Studies
SOG	Society of Genealogists
station	where the district officers lived
suttee/sati	Hindu practice of a widowed woman immolating herself on her husband's funeral pyre; banned in Bengal 1829
thuggee	Hindu cult, associated with murders and attacks
tiffin	luncheon
TNA	The National Archives
Uncovenanted	those who had not entered into a covenant with the ICS (see 'covenanted' above)
Writer	civil servant
zemindar	landowner

British Library IOR Series

B	Minutes of the EIC's Directors and Proprietors 1599–1858
C	Council of India Minutes and Memoranda 1858–1947
D	Minutes and Memoranda etc of General Committees and Offices of the EIC 1700–1858
E	EIC General Correspondence 1602–1859
F	Board of Control General Records 1784–1858
G	Factory Records *c*1595–1858
H	Home Miscellaneous Series *c*1600–*c*1900
I	Records relating to other Europeans in India etc 1475–1824
J	Haileybury Records 1749–1857
L/AG	Accountant General's Records
L/F	Financial Department Records *c*1800–1948

L/MAR	Marine Department Records 1600–1879
L/MED	Medical Boards Records c1920–c1960
L/MIL	Military Department Records 1708–1957
L/P&J	Public & Judicial Department Records 1795–1950
L/PO	Private Office Papers c1858–1948
L/PWD	Public Works Department Records c1839–1931 including bridges, canals, civil aviation, civil engineering, Eastern Mail service, Fisheries, Forestry, Indo-European Telegraph Department, Irrigation, Military Works, Municipal engineering works, ports and harbours, Post Office and postal services, Public buildings and government houses, railways, roads, RIEC, Telegraphs, Wireless telegraphy
L/S&G	Services and General Department Records c1920–c1970
L/WS	War Staff Papers 1921–51
M	Burma Office Records 1932–48
MSS Eur	European Manuscripts, including personal papers of British Indians of all classes and occupations
N	Returns of Baptisms, Marriages, Burials &c 1698–1969
O	Biographical Series 1702–1948
P	Proceedings and Consultations of the Government of India and of the Presidencies and Provinces 1702–1945
Q	Commission, Committee and Conference Records c1895–1947
R	Records transferred later through official channels
V	Official Publications c1760–1957
W, X, Y	Map Collections c1700–1960
Z	Registers and Indexes c1700–1950

CHRONOLOGY OF THE BRITISH IN INDIA

1600	Queen Elizabeth I gives a Royal Charter to 'the Company of Merchants of London trading into the East Indies' establishing the East India Company
1612	EIC wins the Battle of Swally Factory built at Surat
1640	Origins of the Madras Presidency laid when Fort St George is built
1647	EIC had twenty-three factories and ninety British employees
1650	EIC becomes independent of the Crown
1652–74	Three Anglo-Dutch wars
1654	Poplar (East India) Chapel built in London
1668	Factory established at Bombay
1669	Creation of the Bengal Pilot Service
1670	Charles II grants the EIC powers to buy land, mint money, raise its own army, make war and peace, and rule over the land it acquires
1685	Canton opens its ports to foreign traders
1687	Bombay Presidency established
1689	William of Orange crowned King William III of Great Britain, creating an Anglo-Dutch merger
1690	EIC begins controlling the Fort at Sutanuti (later Calcutta) – origins of the Bengal Presidency
1699	EIC establishes a trading base at Canton
1707	Union of Parliaments with Scotland
1756	Incident at the Black Hole of Calcutta
1756–63	Seven Years War (Europe)
1757	Battle of Plassey; Robert Clive becomes Governor of Bengal
1758–59	Siege of Madras
1769–73	Bengal Famine

1773	EIC Charter due for renewal; applies for loan from British Government; Regulating Act; First Governor-General, Warren Hastings
1782	Military Orphan Society founded
1783–4	Bengal Famines
1784	Board of Control established by the East India Act
1791	Cornwallis legislates against Eurasians
1793	Permanent settlement by Cornwallis of Bengal's land revenue
1795–6	Britain takes the Cape Colony
1795–1801	Malacca and the Spice Islands
1796	Dutch East India Company settlements in Ceylon annexed to the Presidency of Madras
1798–9	4th Anglo-Mysore War; Britain establishes military rule in Mysore
1799–1815	Napoleonic Wars
1801	EIC opens an oft-visited Museum and Library at its vast headquarters at East India House in Leadenhall Street, London
1803–05	2nd Anglo-Maratha War
1806	EIC opens the East India Docks in London
1810	EIC captures the Spice Islands of Amboyna, Banda & Ternate
1813	EIC monopoly ends A bishop and three archdeacons appointed to India for the first time
1814	Treaty of Paris: EIC cedes Spice Islands back to the Dutch
1815	Britain rules Ceylon
1817–18	3rd Anglo-Maratha (Pindari) War – Britain defeats the Maratha Confederacy
1819	EIC secures Singapore
1826	Anglo-Dutch Treaty recognizes EIC control of Penang, Singapore and Malacca
1820s	Tea is found growing in Assam
1830	Creation of the Indian Navy
1830s	Overland route to India established (via Egypt)
1833	Governor-General's control extends to all British India; EIC's trading monopoly abolished
1834	EIC Mercantile Marine abolished
1839	EIC conquers Aden

	Indian tea first sold in London
1842	Bundela Rising/Rebellion
1843	EIC conquers Sind
1845	East India Railway Company is formed
1851	Census of Bombay (some survives)
1853	First passenger train journey in India
1857–8	Indian Mutiny
1858	Government of India Act – creation of the India Office; end of EIC rule in India
1859	Creation of the Indian Army (restructuring of the armed forces)
1864	Civil registration begins in Calcutta
1865	Civil registration of deaths begins in Bombay
	Civil registration begins in Burma
1869	Suez Canal opens
1870	Telegraph lines connected between Britain and India
	A single railway line links Bombay to Calcutta
	Civil registration begins in Madras
1872	Registration of births in Bombay begins
1875	Britain becomes a minority shareholder in the Suez Company
1876–8	Great Famine
1876	Eurasian and Anglo-India Association established in Bengal
1877	Queen Victoria declared Empress of India
	HM Indian Marine is formed
1878–80	2nd Afghan War
1879	Anglo-India and Domiciled European Association of Southern India founded
1882	Egyptian Campaign
1885	Sudan Campaign
	General Act of the Conference of Berlin formalizes European imperialism
1887	Nurses are attached to the Indian Army for the first time
1888	Viceregal Lodge built at Simla
1892	Royal Indian Marine
1899–1900	Famine
1909	Morely-Minto reforms
1911	Transfer of national capital from Calcutta to New Delhi

1914–18	First World War
1916	Annie Besant founds the Indian Home Rule League
1917	Russian Revolution
1919	Government of India Act
	Amritsar Massacre
	3rd Afghan War
1920	India High Commission established in London
	Mohandas 'Mahatma' Gandhi begins campaign of non-violent civil disobedience
1921	Montague-Chelmsford reforms
1927	Simon Commission
1930	Civil registration now includes the whole of Bengal
1931	168,000 British in India
1935	Royal Indian Navy
	Government of India Act
1937	Separation of Burma from India
1939–45	Second World War
1941	Japan enters the war
1942	Japan invades Singapore and Burma
	Indian National Congress passes the 'Quit India' resolution
	Women's Auxiliary Corps (WAC[I]) established
1943	Bengal Famine
	Subhas Chandra Bose receives command of the Indian National Army (INA)
1945	INA surrenders
1946	Day of Action Day leads to the Great Calcutta Killings
15 August 1947	India becomes independent of Britain and Pakistan is born

Chapter 1

GETTING STARTED

Since the beginning of the seventeenth century, millions of records have been created about the lives of Britons and Anglo-Indians who lived and worked in and around India. Although this book details many records that survive in archives around the world, you may find a surprising number of useful records at home.

When researching any ancestors it is necessary to establish who you are tracing and where. Unfortunately, researching ancestors who lived in British India can be fraught with problems. Thus, the more clues you have before you begin, the easier the search will be. This chapter will give an overview of what is available on the internet, and explore gathering data from personal and family records. It will also introduce the India Office Records at the British Library, and highlight relevant material held elsewhere, in other libraries and archives.

Name Your Ancestors

Begin by making a list of all your family members who ever lived in British India. Include siblings and spouses – even former spouses, as each brings their own clues. If you are lucky, you may find a complete family tree, replete in baptism, marriage and burial dates, and full addresses for each of your ancestors' homes.

However, for most researchers it will be necessary to search through cupboards, suitcases, attics and lofts for any or all of the following:

- Medals
- Diaries
- Official papers
- Photographs
- Passports
- Letters
- Birth, marriage and death certificates
- Religious documents (e.g. baptism records)

Muriel Collett, National Games Bombay, 1940. (personal collection of Valmay Young)

- Cemetery records
- Wills and probate records

Collate
After gathering everything together and sorting through, take useful notes. Draw as many pedigree charts as necessary, to fit in all the relatives, and ensure the charts include full dates and place names for birth/baptism, marriage and death/burial.

Also create a list of dates: a basic chronology of the main events in your family's history should help to provide clarity in the later stages of your research.

Geography

Maps are important for understanding where your ancestors lived. The boundaries of the India you are researching need to be identified because the India with which the East India Company had links in the seventeenth century was very different from that of 1948. These changing borders of India, and of British control there, can be found in contemporary maps, atlases, libraries or on the internet. Using copies, plot exactly where your ancestors lived. You may be surprised at how far they

2

travelled, often for reasons of work. In summer the offices of government would travel hundreds of miles to escape the heat. It may be useful to visit the Historical Maps of India website at http://homepages.rootsweb.ancestry.com/~poyntz/India/maps.html.

Map of India showing the Average Temperature During the Hot Season (March to May inclusive); During the Cold Season (November to February inclusive). (A Handbook For Travellers To India, Burma and Ceylon (1929))

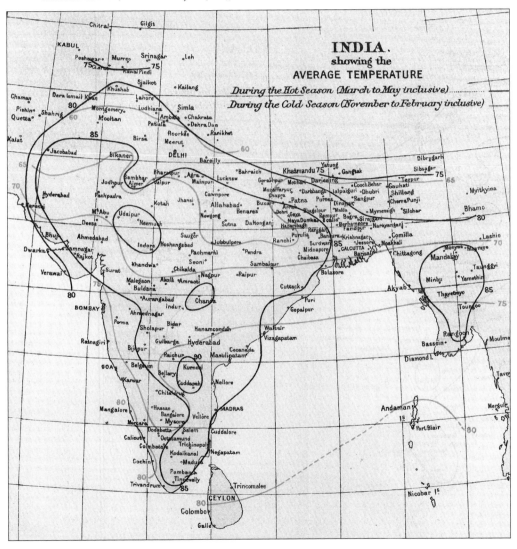

The area covered by this book includes modern-day India, Pakistan, Bangladesh and Burma (now Myanmar). Other areas that you might encounter in India-related records are St Helena, Iraq, Iran (formerly Persia), Aden, Kuwait, Sri Lanka (formerly Ceylon), Singapore, Malacca, Penang Prince of Wales Island, Java, Sumatra (Bencoolen/Fort Marlborough), and China (Macao & Whampoa) – in fact, most places east of the Cape of Good Hope.

One term that you will often encounter in contemporary records is the reference to Presidencies, or administrative areas. As official records are often arranged by Presidency, it is useful to know in which of these your ancestors lived, and when. From the seventeenth century, Britain's trading settlements in India centred on the three Presidency towns of Calcutta, Madras and Bombay. The Presidency of Madras originated from the construction of Fort St George in 1640; the Presidency of Bombay emerged from the East India Company's headquarters moving from Surat to Bombay in 1687; and the Bengal Presidency originated in 1690. Each exported a number of commodities.

As the Company gained more land, the area of control of each Presidency grew. This created three vast Presidencies in the west, east and south of India. A governor administered each of these from the Presidency towns by the mid-eighteenth century. Governors taxed the population to fund the three Presidential armies of Europeans and Indian *sepoys* (Indian soldiers in the service of the British). These armies were used to protect trade, and to help extend the boundaries of British control in India. Of the three Presidencies, Bengal was by far the largest and thus its records can be the most time-consuming to search.

Place names
One complication of researching British India is the problem of place names. Names have been altered from the maps your ancestors used, and while Calcutta is recognizable as modern-day Kolkata, not everywhere is as straightforward. The other former Presidency towns of Madras and Bombay are now known as Chennai and Mumbai. However, Calcutta was previously known as Fort William, and Madras as Fort St George. Spelling often varies, particularly in the numerous copies of records sent 'Home' to the East India Company (and later the India Office) in London. In order to familiarize you with the terms you will encounter in your research, this book uses the contemporary names throughout.

Make a note of each place mentioned in as much detail as possible. This will help with identification, and finding full addresses. There are also clues in the names of churches, houses or streets. The names of the Presidencies may be included, or perhaps Burma or (rarely) Ceylon.

When you have everything organized, your ancestors identified, and places where they lived marked on a map, you may wish to contact other members of your family. There may be elderly relatives with whom you are in contact, or you could find more distant family through websites, like http://www.genesreunited.co.uk, http://www.lostcousins.com, www.geni.com and http://trees.ancestry.co.uk

An alternative way of collaborating with those who are researching the same family or same area of interest as you is to ask questions or contribute suggestions to an online forum. One of the most useful for discussing British Indian ancestors is the INDIA mailing list at http://lists.rootsweb.ancestry.com/index/intl/IND/INDIA.html.

Online Resources

Once you know who you are looking for and where, you can move on to books relating to the British in India, and online indexes to archived documents. Such indexes are invaluable for locating ancestors throughout history.

Some records can be searched online. You may find it easier to work through the following databases at home or in your local library before spending time and money on visiting more distant archives.

Vital records: births, marriages & deaths
Unlike in England and Wales, where civil registration was introduced in 1837 (with compulsory registration from 1875), or Scotland where registration was compulsory for all from 1855, there was no compulsory registration of births, marriages and deaths in India. Registration began in Calcutta in 1864; in Madras in 1870; and 1865 for deaths, 1872 for births in Bombay. Registration in Burma began in 1865, and for the whole of Bengal in 1930. Where examples of civil registration do exist, they appear in the main from the 1920s, and can be a useful accompaniment to a surviving religious record. Births and deaths should be recorded if the event took place in a hospital rather than at home. Copies of the registration records may be held in India at the respective Registrar's Office.

For most vital events in British India, however, researchers need to rely on Christian records of baptisms, marriages and deaths. Many of these are held in India Office Records at the British Library.

EXTRACT FROM THE REGISTER OF MARRIAGES

KEPT AT

ST. PATRICK'S CHURCH, BANGALORE.

———

When Married	28th August 1943.	
Christian name of the Parties	Robert Lionel.	Emily.
Surname ,, ,, ,,	Gunther.	Upshon.
Age ., ,, ,,	29.	24.
Condition ,, ,, .,	Bachelor.	Spinster.
Rank or Profession ,, ,,	I. E.	
Residence at the time of Marriage	Khargpur.	Bangalore.
Father's Name and Surname	Robert Francis Gunther.	Robert William Upshon.
By Banns or License	L i c e n s e.	
Signatures of the Parties	R. L. Gunther.	Emily Upshon.
Signatures of two or more Witnesses present	R. W. Upshon.	F. Coombes.
Signature of the Minister by whom the ceremony is performed	L. Vampeene.	

TRUE EXTRACT,

BANGALORE,

Date: 28/8/'43.

Catholic Chaplain,

Marriage Certificate of Robert Lionel Gunther & Emily Upshon. (Noel Gunther)

However, it is also possible to glean vital records information from other sources. Some indexes have been compiled with data taken from all of the above records.

One of the most basic resources in the search for British Indian ancestors is the British Library's Indian Office Family History at http://indiafamily.bl.uk/UI. This database can be searched by keyword, name or place and covers more than 300,000 births, baptisms, marriages, deaths and burials in the India Office Records (IOR). The details were taken from a large card index that used to be held in AAS (OIR.920.054) and includes the names of some entries from IOR biographical sources, such as R.H. Phillimore, *Historical Records of the Survey of India*; Basil St G. Drennan (ed.), *The Keble College Centenary Register*; V.C.P. Hodson, *List of the Officers of the Bengal Army, 1758–1834*; C.H. Malden (ed.), *List of burials at Madras from 1660 to 1746, compiled from the register of St Mary's Church, Fort St George*; George William de Rhé-Philipe, *Inscriptions on Christian*

Wedding photograph of Robert Gunther & Emily Upshon. (Noel Gunther)

tombs or monuments; *Bengal Past and Present*; and the *Asiatic Journal*. Once an entry is found via this online index, the original source can be consulted in AAS. Some churches include documents on their own websites. For example, see http://stmaryschurchpune.org/archives1html and http://www.allsaintschurch.co.in.

The main series of baptisms, marriages and burials is indexed in the N series in the British Library (see Chapter 7). This series of records is being digitized. It is searchable online at www.findmypast.co.uk. The family history search site of the Church of Jesus Christ of the Latter-Day Saints (LDS), https://www.familysearch.org contains many of the ecclesiastical records in its indexes to Indian records (using the option 'Asia and the Middle East'), and includes details such as the names of parents for a baptism or the exact place of burial. This site can be searched by name or browsed by location. Once a record is found, the relevant microfilm reference at the British Library can be located via the index on the FIBIS website (http://bit.ly/fieyWW).

Photograph of Robert P. Gunther & Clara Lydia Platel. (Noel Gunther)

There are also records from the Colombo District Dutch Reformed Church in Sri Lanka.

The LDS Church has microfilmed the registers of some parishes whose records are not held at the British Library. As well as these, LDS Family History Centres hold copies of many AAS microfilms which you can consult locally. Indexes of these are available at FIBIwiki http://wiki.fibis.org. Discover where your nearest Family History Centre is by checking on https://library.familysearch.org.

Other available vital records include the indexes for Overseas Births, Marriages and Deaths 1761–2005 at www.findmypast.co.uk including GRO regimental, consular and marine indexes. For Scottish overseas records, see www.scotlandspeople.gov.uk.

www.thegenealogist.co.uk is useful for nonconformist vital records and UK censuses (which identify people born in India).

http://indiaman.com is a genealogy and history magazine about the British in the Indian subcontinent with an online database. Back copies can be found at SOG.

An index of names mentioned in birth, marriage and death announcements can be found at www.honesteastindiaco.com/names.html.

For information on those who have migrated from South Asia to the UK, see http://www.movinghere.org.uk.

A compilation of websites on Asia and Pacific genealogy is available at http://www.cyndislist.com/asia.

Families in British India Society (FIBIS)

Family history societies are always useful for researchers seeking to make contacts or further their research. For those tracing their ancestors in British India, FIBIS is essential.

The society's website (http://www.new.fibis.org) is one of the best online resources available in this field, with a large and continually growing searchable database (up to three-quarter million records so far) of free material. This includes vital records, service records, directories, cemetery records, military detail and old photographs. Several of these records are featured throughout this book. There is also a members-only section with further sources, a blog on the latest British Indian Family History news, and a social networking area to help you connect with others researching your ancestors. Separately, there are information sites like FIBIwiki (http://www.wiki.fibis.org), which provide data for those studying the background to their ancestors' lives and where users can share details on researching their ancestors in India. The society has published several in-depth guides and books on various aspects of

British Indian history. There is a guide to *Getting the best out of the FIBIS website* (Fact File No. 5) by Valmay Young. The membership is very helpful and active, with contacts and transcribers all over the world, including branches in Australia. They also offer an inexpensive research service for members who are unable to visit London archives as a result of disability or distance. SOG holds past copies of the FIBIS Journal.

A FIBIS member based in Sri Lanka is currently transcribing baptism, marriage and burial details of Europeans in Ceylon.

Explore archives online

As well as online biographical information, newspapers and books, catalogues can help you locate rare letters, diaries and memoirs that may have been written by or mention your ancestors. Access to Archives (A2A) is a useful website which combines catalogues of many local

Jhansi: Val Wardley and Curly Swinbourne, 1942. (personal collection of Valmay Young)

10

records offices and other archives in England and Wales, including much of the catalogue for the India Office Records found by selecting 'British Library' in http://www.nationalarchives.gov.uk/A2A/default.aspx.

The British Library's collection of India Office private papers can be searched online at http://minos1.bl.uk/catalogues/indiaofficeselect/welcome.asp.

The above site also includes access to the catalogue of the India Office paintings, prints, drawings and photographs.

Once a relevant entry is found, the original documents can be ordered and examined in person in the AAS.

Other databases can be searched for India/Asia-related material, such as those of cemeteries, and these will be covered in further chapters.

Newspapers and books

The British Library is an excellent resource for seventeenth- to nineteenth-century newspapers. Its database (http://newspapers.bl.uk/blcs) covers many local and national titles, which can be searched using free-text keywords. Although free to use at the British Library, and in other libraries and archives, the full text of an article from British Newspapers 1800–1900 can only be seen on home computers for a subscription fee. The *Penny Illustrated Paper* and *The Graphic* can be viewed freely (use the 'free content only' option on the search engine), and local libraries may have subscriptions that you can use online as a library member. There are also similar resources that can be found on genealogy websites, such as the index to the *Gentleman's Magazine* 1731–1868 on www.ancestry.co.uk. More than 40 million newspaper images from the British Library's collections are being digitized in partnership with brightsolid Online Publishing over the next ten years. The newspapers are being made available at http://www.britishnewspaperarchive.co.uk.

Another useful resource freely available at the British Library and other major archives is *The Times* Digital Archive 1785–2005, http://www.thetimes.co.uk/tto/archive. Many local libraries also provide free access to this and the *Guardian/Observer* archive, and it is well worth searching for references to named ancestors, places, or events in which they may have been involved. Searching for the names of ships may help to discover more about the passage of your ancestors to India. Again, subscriptions are available for those wishing to search at home.

The FIBIwiki website (see above) contains a number of links to historic Indian newspapers that can be searched online at http://www.wiki.fibis.org/index.php?title=Newspapers and journals online.

Other published indexes and online biographical sources are available within the British Library, the Society of Genealogists, and other major libraries. These vary from small pamphlets to large resources like the *Oxford Dictionary of National Biography* (again, available for a subscription online at home or can be accessed for free via the British Library or local archive and library membership). This can also be found in many libraries in a set of hard copy volumes.

Several internet search engines exist to help you locate useful books:

COPAC http://copac.ac.uk/search – this is a library catalogue, containing roughly 36 million records from the merged online catalogues of many major UK and Irish academic and national libraries, as well as increasing numbers of specialist libraries.

www.archive.org – the Internet archive includes several digitized records relating to the British in India.

http://books.google.com – ancestors' names, graves or residences may be found within contemporary texts, sometimes published online in full.

Most books can be ordered in advance and consulted at the British Library, or a good reference library near where you live.

See also http://scholar.google.com for references to academic articles.

For a similar website based in India, which includes records of the British there, see the Digital Library of India (www.new.dli.ernet.in).

Visiting Archives

Although many records have been digitized, and several more are being put online over the next few years, there are still millions of records in archives around the world that lie dusty and unused. Modern developments have been very helpful to the family historian but to research your ancestor's Indian activities as thoroughly as possible, you will need to use records held in archives – whether in person or through the services of archivists or researchers.

Inside the British Library

The British Library is central to researching the British in India since the main series of family history records are held here. The Library is situated in Euston Road in central London. The Library is vast, giving access to most published English-language material. There are several computer terminals, although most visitors prefer to bring their own laptop and browse the internet via the free public wifi system.

Although the Library is open seven days a week, the Asian and African Studies Reading Room (AAS) is only open Monday to Saturday. There are ramps and lifts for wheelchair users; wheelchairs can be booked in advance.

For detailed queries regarding visiting the British Library (www.bl.uk), contact Tel: +44 (0)20 7412 7332; Textphone: +44 (0)20 7387 0626; Email: visitor-services@bl.uk.

Asian and African Studies Reading Room (AAS). Currently home to the India Office Records (IOR), AAS provides access to a wealth of indexes and masses of original documents. Formerly APAC, previously the Oriental and India Office Collections (OIOC), it holds records on Asia, Islamic North Africa, the Horn of Africa and the Caucasus. These include print and manuscript collections, such as private papers, official publications, journals, newspapers, maps, prints, drawings and photographs.

After using some of the databases mentioned above, it is likely that you will have found references to records that can be consulted in the British Library. The more detailed aspects of the records will be discussed in later chapters. This section introduces you to the most popular records on India in the British Library's collections. Some material can be ordered in advance but there are many open-access indexes, printed transcriptions and copies of original documents freely available on shelves or in microfilm cabinets around AAS.

To enquire about the collections, you can write to the team at the Euston Road address, telephone on +44 (0)20 7412 7873, or online via the question point website http://www.questionpoint.org/crs/servlet/org. oclc.admin.BuildForm?&institution=13430&type=1&language=1.

In order to enter the reading rooms of the British Library, you need to be registered for a Reader Pass. You can do this online but need to take identification and proof of address on your first visit. Full details on registration are available at http://www.bl.uk/reshelp/inrrooms/stp/ register/stpregister.html.

The many records that form the India Office Records (IOR) collection, and which are not open-access, need to be ordered online via Explore the British Library http://www.explore.bl.uk at home or in the reading room, by clicking the 'Request List' link, and then choosing the 'Asia, Pacific and Africa Collections' option. You then need to choose the relevant option from the list of record types. A common mistake is to highlight 'India Office Records' rather than 'Microfilms' if it is a microfilm that is being ordered. Most IOR records will be digitized on Find My Past from 2012 but many other records, such as directories, will only be available in the Reading Room.

Photocopying services are available, and it is possible to print from microfilms and make your own copies from approved books. Many original documents are too delicate or heavy to be self-copied but some may be scanned by reading-room staff. Original material in heavier volumes may be ordered online from the British Library's Imaging Services via http://www.bl.uk/reshelp/atyourdesk/imaging/imaginghome.html.

India Office Records. The India Office Records comprise those of the East India Company (c1600–1858), its Board of Control (1784–1858), the India Office (1858–1948) and the Burma Office (1937–48). Significantly, these records include copies of many Ecclesiastical Returns, especially for the Presidencies of Bengal, Madras and Bombay.

Where no vital record information appears for your ancestor, it is possible to discover more with a little detective work. Using non-standard resources, such as the annual *Thacker's Directory* and other earlier directories, is helpful. Thacker's *Directory of India* is a directory (like the Post Office Directories commonly used by genealogists in Britain) that gives details of Europeans and Indians in India. Details vary over the years but the cities of Calcutta, Madras, Bombay, Allahabad, Lahore, Simla and Rangoon are all covered. It also includes an almanac, army lists, civil lists, railway and business lists, a newspaper directory and general information. Later editions include a street directory of Calcutta. The indexes of residents are split into Europeans and Indians and mainly cover people in senior positions. Information on other areas can be found in the gazetteers on the open shelves.

Other collections in the British Library Records & Resources. The only genealogically useful census record of Europeans in India that exists for this period is the 1851 Bombay Census. The original census is held in IOR/P/350/59/7531 and an index can be found online at http://valmayukuk.tripod.com/id32.html.

Some deaths in India were reported in Britain, particularly in the *Gentleman's Magazine* and *The Times* (London). Almanacs & Directories for the three Presidencies also contain death notices. Do note that many of the early issues of the Indian directories are not indexed, and thus it may take time to search through them.

Obituaries are an excellent resource for learning about an ancestor's life and character. Records containing these may be found via the resources mentioned above, and in *British Library's Newspapers 1600–1900*

(Gale databases), which can be useful for finding obituaries in lesser-known publications. Hodson's *Officers of the Bengal Army 1758–1834*; *Who Was Who*, and Frederick Boase's *Modern English Biography* can also help locate dates of death for senior military or political personnel, and celebrated British people in India.

Europeans were employed in a variety of occupations. The India Office records contain information for surgeons, veterinary surgeons, nurses, mercantile mariners, advocates, journalists, missionaries and engineers, among others. People with these jobs may also be found in the directories.

English-Language newspapers published in India

AAS holds a *Handlist of Western Language South Asian Newspapers Held on Microfilm* (of which most are in English). This list is arranged alphabetically by title, and lists more than 200 newspapers covering a variety of dates. The British Library does not always hold all issues produced but the holdings for each title are given in brackets. Sadly none of these are indexed.

Local newspapers could mention the death of a relative who died in suspicious circumstances. Reports of inquests may be discovered in newspapers that cover court proceedings, and obituaries and death notices are included in many titles. Also if your ancestor was well-known in India or suffered a death through murder or an accident, it is worth checking for a more detailed news report for up to two weeks after the date of the fatality. *The Times of India* 1838–2002 is available online via ProQuest http://www.proquest.com/assets/literature/products/databases/hnp-india.pdf.

In order to find the newspaper most likely to mention your ancestor, it is important to check the place of publication. By checking *Place Names in India* (IOR/Z/N/126) in the reading room, you can discover in which Presidency your ancestor lived. This is useful as most newspapers were published in the three Presidential cities. Some titles, such as *Allen's Indian Mail* (1843; 1845–91) and *Indiaman* (1914–17) were published in London, and so were not India-specific in their coverage. *The Englishman* (published in Calcutta) included English news alongside Indian events. However, some such as the *Bihar Herald* (1913–15; 1927; 1933–61) were published in Patna, covered a smaller area, and are therefore more likely to include local crimes and incidents.

The *Manhattan* (1881–1950), or the *Poona Observer* (1876–77; 1878–1906) based in Poona may be useful for deaths of officers or soldiers at the large military *cantonment*.

Other London Archives

The National Archives

The National Archives at Kew (TNA) holds several useful series of records, particularly on the British Army. Some of these records have been uploaded to the web and can be consulted via www.findmypast. co.uk, www.ancestry.co.uk and http://discovery.nationalarchives.gov. uk (Discovery). The National Archives website includes research guides to family history and a check of a relative s name on the catalogue may prove useful. Searching the catalogue via Discovery and ordering as many documents as possible in advance of a visit will help to maximize research time once there. Several useful TNA records are also available to browse via Discovery in the Digital Microfilms section. These records are not indexed.

Military records are examined in more detail in Chapter 5.

Society of Genealogists

The India shelves (shelf-mark IND) of the Society of Genealogists (SOG) are packed with rare books, gazetteers and typescripts on the history of the British in India, as well as long runs of the *East India register and directory, Indian Army List, Indian Navy List* and Civil Service Lists. There are personal accounts of families who lived in India on the family history shelves, plus genealogies (many in IND/G 73), gazetteers, transcripts of births, marriages, deaths and monumental inscriptions. Further information can be found at www.sog.org.uk.

Lieutenant Colonel H. Kendal Percy-Smith began what is now known as the Percy-Smith Index in 1933. Today, it contains eight volumes of births, marriages and deaths of British people in India *c*1780–1857 (IND/R 1–8) taken from publications like *Asiatic Journal*, *Bengal Directory* and registers. His index to IOR marriages covers 1698–1900 Bengal, Madras, Bombay, Burma, St Helena, Singapore, Penang, Bencoolen and Macao.

National Army Museum Library, London

This holds the card index of Major V.C.P. Hodson. This builds on the information held in Hodson's *List of Officers of the Bengal Army*, in that the cards include officers of the Bombay and Madras armies, Civil Servants, Officers of the East Indiamen, plus chaplains and clergymen. The Library also holds further card indexes by Percy-Smith. More details can be found at http://www.national-army-museum.ac.uk/oldResearch/files/tscInfo1. pdf and in 'The India-related holdings of the National Army Museum' by Marion Harding and Jenny Spencer-Smith in FIBIS journal no. 15.

National Maritime Museum

The National Maritime Museum (NMM) holds the world's largest maritime collection. It contains the Traders Gallery, housing objects from across Asia and the Indian Ocean relating to the history of the East India Company. See www.rmg.co.uk.

The Women in India index (from the National Maritime Museum) is currently being digitized for www.findmypast.co.uk. There is also a surname index to Anglo-Indian research correspondence 1949–50 (IND/G 112A).

School of Oriental and African Studies (SOAS)

The SOAS of the University of London has an extensive archive of manuscripts and papers relating to South Asia, with a strong focus on the activities of a number of major British missionary societies, and of individual missionaries. Cameras are allowed in its reading rooms. Its archive catalogue can be explored at http://squirrel.soas.ac.uk/dserve (website: www.soas.ac.uk).

You may also find the collections of several museums useful. Some specific museums are mentioned later in the book but one useful for discovering general history on British India is the British Empire and Commonwealth Museum, which is currently relocating from Bristol to London: http://www.empiremuseum.co.uk.

Archives Elsewhere in the UK

There are several other archives and libraries that hold British Indian material. It is sensible to check their catalogues and to contact the relevant archive before visiting. Of these, the following are recommended:

Bodleian Library, Oxford (http://www.bodleian.ox.ac.uk/bodley) holds a number of collections on Britain's imperial and colonial history 1600–1800, including the Rawlinson manuscripts, the papers of George Macartney and the mercantile papers of John Palmer. For Asian material, see its Rhodes House Library of Commonwealth Studies.

Centre of South Asian Studies, Cambridge holds valuable collections of papers and memoirs in its South Asian Archives; details are available on its website http://www.s-asian.cam.ac.uk/overview.html. The Oral History Collection can be listened to or transcripts read online at http://www.s-asian.cam.ac.uk/audio.html, and some of the Centre's large archive of films on life in South Asia (1911–56) can be viewed at http://www.s-asian.cam.ac.uk/films.html.

At 4,000 volumes, the **National Library of Scotland (NLS)**'s India Papers collection is one of the largest collections of publications on the British Indian state outside the British Library. The material was deposited under a scheme administered by the India Office, although some was published in the UK on behalf of Indian governments. Others have been donated from various sources or purchased, such as the composite volumes assembled by George Smith and Joseph Owen. The Minto Papers (the 1st Earl having been Governor-General of India, 1807–13, and the 4th Earl was Viceroy from 1905–10) include some early material but most records date from after 1857 to around 1920. More information on this can be found on the NLS websites http://www.nls.uk/collections, http://digital.nls.uk/jma and http://www.nls.uk/family-history/india-papers.

India

There are, of course, many useful resources in India itself. As with all records, there may be a problem with what has survived. Also, not all records are contained in accessible archives. Many churches continue to hold their own registers, for example. It may help to have contacts in the area who can speak with church representatives on your behalf.

The most popular and accessible resource in India is probably the National Archives of India in New Delhi. They hold a wealth of material on India between 1600 and 1948, including public records, private papers, oriental records and manuscripts at http://nationalarchives.nic.in/writereaddata/html_en_files/html/NAIH_Lib.html. Several of these records include information on British Indians of all backgrounds and social classes. For those researching British India, some of the most useful series among the Public Records are the Home Department Miscellaneous (1680–1932), Public/General/Home Department (1764–1879; 1881–1946), the Legislative Department (1777–1859; 1869–1947) and the Military Department (1756–1969).

Do note that foreign nationals are required to submit a letter of introduction from their sponsoring University/Institution as well as a letter of introduction from the diplomatic mission of their country in India, although the archivists do respond to email.

Other useful institutions are the Delhi Archives (records of the government of the National Capital Territory of Delhi http://nationalarchives.nic.in), the Indian Historical Record Commission, and local archives (such as that of Tamil Nadu at http://www.tanap.net/content/archives/archives.cfm?ArticleID=202), and the Carey Library at Serampore (http://www.seramporecollege.org/theology/clri.htm). In Kolkata there are a number of useful archives, including that of the High Court of Calcutta (http://calcuttahighcourt.nic.in), the National Library (http://www.nationallibrary.gov.in), the West Bengal State Archives, and the Victoria Memorial Records Room (http://www.victoriamemorial-cal.org).

For a full list of Indian state archives, see: http://nationalarchives.nic.in/writereaddata/html_en_files/html/StatesList.html.

To arrange local searches in India, contact the Foreign and Commonwealth Office, Nationality and Passport Section, Consulate Directorate, King Charles Street, London SW1A 2AH (tel: 0207 008 0186), http://www.co.gov.uk/en).

Chapter 2

HISTORY OF THE BRITISH IN INDIA: THE EAST INDIA COMPANY (EIC)

The Pepper ... is the most necessary Spice ... It is not to be had but from India; and if the English had no East-India-trade, it must be purchased from the Hollander ...

Thomas Papillon, Sir Josiah Child, *The East-India-trade a most profitable trade to the kingdom &c* (1680)

Origins of the East India Company (EIC)

By the beginning of the twentieth century, Britain controlled 943,000 square miles of the Indian subcontinent and ruled over its 226 million people.[1] The British Isles, meanwhile, covered a mere 90,504 square miles,[2] and in 1900 had a population of only 36,686,000. So how did such a small kingdom come to rule over a land mass of more than ten times its own, and a population of over six times its size?

The answer lies in trade. Britain's entire presence in India and all that it came to own began with a small band of traders: the East India Company (EIC), and its administrators and military protectors. However, the East India Company did not develop out of a desire to create a great empire. Initially, there was no focus on gaining territory; its early officers simply wanted to profit from buying and selling.

Trade with India grew out of Europeans' exploratory sea voyages in the fifteenth and sixteenth centuries. During their travels they acquired trading posts around the world; the Asian trading posts, with their proximity to the Silk Route, were particularly valuable. Sailors, traders and pirates all made money from silk, spices, fine china and precious metals. Many of these sailed from British ports.

On 31 December 1600, Queen Elizabeth I gave a Royal Charter to 'the Company of Merchants of London trading into the East Indies', granting it a monopoly on this trade for fifteen years. From its base in Leadenhall Street, London, the EIC set off to make a great profit.

At first spices (including pepper, nutmeg, mace, cloves and cinnamon) were the chief trading commodity from the east (particularly as the English wished to import pepper at a far cheaper price than that bought from the Dutch), although the EIC also traded in carpets, perfumes and precious stones.

The rival Dutch East India Company had been formed from a group of merchants who had set off for Java earlier than the EIC, in 1596. The 'Dutch United East Indies Company' (VOC) lasted from 1602 until 1796 but initially the Dutch dominated trade with the spice islands of Moluccas and Bandas (now Indonesia). If your ancestor travelled to the Molucca Islands, or died there, you may wish to search records of the Dutch East Indies on the Dutch website http://www.roosjeroos.nl. Several Britons are recorded on the site, including William Robinson Esq. Sub Treasurer and Collector of Customs at Batavia (now Jakarta), whose death was recorded there in 1815. Using the dates on the website, many of those recorded can be followed up in obituaries in *The Times* or the *Gentleman's Magazine*.

The EIC's initial trading post in India was at Surat (in Gujarat), a centre for the spice trade, where a factory was built in 1612. Four years later, the governor of Surat controlled all of the company's activities along the western coast of India. Fierce competition between the two companies led inevitably to the price of spices being reduced. Although the VOC attempted to stop the EIC from trading directly in spice, the English bypassed this by trading Indian cloth out of Madras in exchange for spice bought from other countries in the East Indies. Eventually, the conflict led to three Anglo-Dutch wars between 1652 and 1674 over control of the sea routes out of Western Europe. The English fared so badly that they lost their trading posts in West Africa.

As the importance and value of other commodities grew and altercations with the Dutch became more severe, the EIC focused less on spice. Its trading centre was moved to Bombay after a factory had been established there in 1668. By 1687, Bombay had also replaced Surat as the main west coast Presidency town of the EIC. Records of the factory in Surat can be found in series IOR/G/36 Surat (1616–1804).

The EIC's trade had been helped by the support of the ruling Mughals, who had approved its business since the British defeated the anti-Muslim Portuguese in the 1612 Battle of Swally, near Surat. In return the

English gave the Mughal Emperor Jahangir luxury goods from Europe. By 1647 the Company had twenty-three factories (fortified trading posts) and employed ninety Britons in India. More information on the factories can be found in records at the British Library, some of which are held on microfilm in series IOR/G (Factory Records). The records detail the work of the Company's civil servants in establishing factories and promoting trade in the East, and they show how the EIC overcame the opposition of the native businessmen and dealt with their rivals, the Portuguese and the Dutch.

Eventually, in 1650 the Company gained its independence from the Crown. In 1670, Charles II granted the EIC powers to buy land, mint money, raise its own army, make war and peace, and rule over the land it acquired.

At the end of the 1680s, the EIC's luck changed when Prince William of Orange was invited to become King William III of Great Britain. The coronation of this Dutch prince as King of England created an Anglo-Dutch merger, and enabled the EIC to grow stronger. Again, luck was on the Company's side when the trade was divided. While the Dutch received the soon-to-wane spice trade and Indonesia, the English received the textile trade with India, which was set to boom.

There was no Great Britain at this stage; the Union of Parliaments with Scotland was to occur in 1707. A separate Scottish company was established in 1695: 'the Company of Scotland Trading to Africa and the Indies.' However, this soon faded from view in the wake of the mighty EIC, in which many Scots became governors, senior civil servants, and surgeons.

In 1699, the EIC began trading with Canton in China whence came tea, silks, porcelain and, most controversially, opium. Besides these goods, the EIC was now bringing home calicoes, cushions, curtains, cotton, muslin gowns, chintz, Bengal silk, taffeta and spices to England. Indian textiles, particularly cotton cloth woven by Indian weavers, became very popular in Europe. The fabrics were cheap, washable and lightweight, and were imported in bulk to be sold as dresses and furnishings. Cotton even affected the locations of the Company's main settlements, as cotton textiles were most readily available for export in Calcutta, Madras and Bombay.

The popularity of Indian cloth in Britain had been evident as early as 1663 when Pepys recorded in his diary entry of 5 September: 'my wife, and I to Cornhill, and after many tryalls bought my wife a chintz, that is, a painted Indian callico, for to line her new study, which is very pretty.' He went on to write, 'I did inform myself well in things relating to the

East Indys ... and the inconsiderablenesse of the place of Bombaim [Bombay], if we had had it.' Just five years later Britain did have it, and the Presidency it was to become was certainly not inconsiderable.

During the seventeenth century, the British established factories at their three main centres of trade. These were:

(i) Fort St George (the city that later became Madras, the seat of the Madras Presidency) was built by the British in 1640.

(ii) Bombay (acquired from Portugal as part of the dowry of Catherine of Braganza on her marriage to Charles II), which replaced Surat as the trade centre of western India in 1668.

(iii) Fort at Sutanuti on the River Hooghly (now Hugli), at the mouth of the Bay of Bengal, which was controlled by the EIC from 1690. After merging with two other villages, this fort became known as Calcutta.

In the seventeenth century it took six months to reach Calcutta from England. Due to the operation of the monsoon trade winds, ships could only leave in the spring and return in autumn. The advantage of this for the EIC's trade was that the length of time involved made it very difficult for other companies to compete. However, it would also have been difficult for the EIC to grow without the presence of the so-called 'interlopers'. These were former EIC employees who had left the company and set up their own small trading businesses. Although their activities reduced the EIC's monopoly on trade, they also helped to increase the number of products that could reach London, thus maintaining a market in Britain for Indian goods.

Success of Nabobs who made their fortune in India

Nabob is a corruption of the princely title Nawab. The term nabob was first used to mean 'governor' but later defined a deputy. However, in popular terminology it was used to describe EIC men who achieved great wealth and prominence. The riches of the EIC had grown enormously as the Company profited from the textile trade at the expense of the Indian workers. Of those senior Company officers who survived the climate and illnesses of the distant land, many nabobs returned home with vast fortunes. Thomas Pitt, Robert Clive and Warren Hastings were all nabobs; they made their fortune in India and returned their money to Britain where they built grand houses. Thomas 'Diamond' Pitt (1653–1726) was the son of a Dorset rector. However, the great wealth he accumulated during his time as variously merchant, interloper and President of Madras enabled him to buy land that led to a seat in the House of Commons. Thanks to this seat, his grandson, William Pitt, was able to become Prime Minister. Several of Thomas's letters can be found among the East India Company Letter Books at the British Library in IOR/E/3/84–111 (1626–1753). These records and the EIC General Correspondence of IOR/E can be searched by name on A2A. Such correspondence gives an insight into life for the British in general in seventeenth-century India.

A later threat to the EIC came from France, which had its own East India Company: *La Compagnie des Indes Orientales* (CdI). The French differed from the English and the Dutch in that their aim was to gain territory, not trade. Their base was at Pondicherry (just south of the British Fort St George), and from here they sought to force the EIC out of the Madras area. This resulted in the 1747 Siege of Madras, which the British successfully held, thanks to extra support from the Royal Navy. In 1748 the French finally let go of Madras. From 1756–63 many of the countries of Europe were engaged in the Seven Years War. With an increase in the size of the Navy, Britain was able to capture all the French bases in India (including Pondicherry) by 1762. The EIC, with its private armies and the help of British military powers, had proved that it could see off competitors. To search the civil records of those based at Pondicherry, see the website of the Archives Nationales d'Outre-Mer (ANOM) http://anom.archivesnationales.culture.gouv.fr/caomec2.

Mughal Empire

Delhi was the residence of the Muslim Mughal emperors who had ruled much of India from the sixteenth century, and was thus the centre of Indian political power. They controlled Bengal, which was India's richest province. While the Mughal Empire was strong, the EIC's hold on India was weak. However, the Emperor – swayed by bribes, negotiations, begging, grovelling etc – gave permission to the EIC to trade. In order to continue to trade, the EIC civil servants had to continue with the bribes, grovelling and treaties. This led to the creation of an effective diplomatic corps within the company. Information on diplomats at this time can be found in surviving diaries or letters, some of which are held in the European manuscripts section of AAS in series MSS Eur, and in the Cambridge South Asian Archive.

As Company employees began to tire of this tedious diplomacy, they were eager to take advantage when the Emperor's power began to slip in the 1740s. Attacks from the Persians (1739) and the Afghans (after 1740) and the creation of their own mini-kingdoms by former Mughal deputies in the provinces led to a power struggle between Indian rulers.

The violence of the conflicts spilled into EIC forts, and the need for a private army increased. The EIC thus raised regiments from India's warrior castes, who were commanded by British officers.

Robert Clive ('Clive of India') 1725–74 and the Black Hole of Calcutta

In the 1760s, EIC civil servant turned military officer, Baron Clive of Plassey, was Governor of Bengal for the second time and the most powerful man in the subcontinent. He was to be known as the 'conqueror of India', yet his fall from grace was severe, and he ended his

Robert Clive, 1st Baron Clive, 1725–74. (from http://en.wikipedia.org/wiki/File@LordClive.jpg)

life by his own hand at the age of just 49. Historians have described Clive variously as cunning, corrupt, crazed, violent and greedy but he is central to the history of the British in India, for without his actions the EIC would never have gained control of India.

The French were as keen as the British to take advantage of weaknesses in the Mughal Empire, and threatened the EIC position. From 1756–63 the British fought the Seven Years War, eventually defeating the French with the might of the EIC Army and the British Navy. It was during one of the longest of these conflicts that Clive came to prominence: he won the siege of Arcot (1751) after commanding the besieged British garrison for fifty days against a Franco-Indian force.

However, it is the Battle of Plassey (Palashi) on 23 June 1757 which is widely regarded as the key point in British Indian history, when the EIC grew from being a mere group of traders to becoming the landowners and empire-builders of the world's first multinational corporation.

Siraj ud-Daulah, *Nawab* of Bengal since 10 April 1756, had been concerned with the EIC's abuse of position and tried to bring the Company under government control. When the EIC refused to fulfil his wishes, Siraj ud-Daulah took the EIC's Kasimbazar factory (3 June 1756) and then one of the Company's main bases, Fort William in Calcutta (20 June 1756). As Siraj ud-Daulah was an ally of the French in the Seven Years War, they backed the *Nawab* when his forces attacked the base.

At Fort William the *Nawab*'s armies captured between sixty and 150 British prisoners. They were imprisoned in a tiny cell, possibly 18ft by 14ft, with few if any windows. It was alleged that most of these prisoners died as a result of the cramped conditions. One survivor, John Zephaniah Holwell (later temporary Governor of Bengal) wrote an account of this, 'A Genuine Narrative of the Deplorable Deaths of the English Gentlemen and others who were suffocated in the Black Hole'. Holwell later returned to Britain, where he died in Pinner, Middlesex in 1798. However, his account has been questioned over the years. More recently it is believed that Holwell embellished the story, and that at most the dead numbered forty-three. This cell became known as the Black Hole of Calcutta, and this incident – and the shocked reaction to it back in Britain – was used by the EIC repeatedly to justify its future aggression.

This notorious episode affected attitudes of British policy-makers and the minds of those who would later live and work in India. The tale was taught in schools and its power should not be underestimated. Holwell gives a list of the victims (also found in Busteed's Appendix to his 1888 *Echoes of Old Calcutta*). More information on those named can be found in military records (L/MIL series), open-access directories and private papers (MSS Eur series) in AAS.

Allegedly, it was to avenge this incident that the then Lieutenant-Colonel Clive and around 3,000 EIC soldiers (most of whom were Indian) attacked the 5,000-strong army of Siraj ud-Daulah and the French. On the day before the battle took place, Clive persuaded Siraj ud-Daulah's rival and uncle, Mir Jafar, to defect to the British side. Thus showing the cunning for which he was later famed, Clive exploited Indian feuds for his own ends.

At the battle, mindful of the effects of rain the British took care to cover their cannon powder. The *Nawab*'s powder was unprotected and spoiled in the heavy downfall of 23 June 1757. Consequently, the *Nawab* lost at least 500 troops, while the EIC lost just twenty-two.

Following the Battle of Plassey, Clive received a £234,000 gift (equivalent to £34 million today) and £27,000 rent from some land *jagirs* granted by Mir Jafar. After the Treaty of Allahabad, granting the EIC administration (*diwani*) of Bengal, Bihar and Orissa by the Mughal ruler, Shah Alam in 1765, Clive became Governor of Bengal, effectively ruling Mughal lands and troops in the province, and proceeded to take 'half of the coin and jewels of greater Bengal'.[3] The Mughals remained important symbolically: Mir Jafar became *Nawab* of Bengal but he was without any real power, and unable to prevent the revenue that should have been coming to him being sent to Britain.

Wars were regular occurrences in these early years as the EIC fought to conquer more lands. Early attempts, such as the First Anglo-Mysore War (1766–69), were failures but the military upheaval had terrible consequences for many in the native population, leading to famine and death.

Some of the profit from taxation was used to finance the EIC's army and to organize the further taxation of the newly-acquired territories (with a population of at least 20 million people). However, the rest made its way to Britain. Bengali farmers were so heavily taxed after the EIC trebled rates and banned rice 'hoarding' that when crops failed they were unable to cope with the grain shortage. The consequent 1769–73 famine resulted in the deaths of almost a third of the population.

This period was the beginning of the 'drain' of Indian wealth to British coffers. Between 1783 and 1793, as Britain conquered more land, the EIC is believed to have taken £1.3 million from India. When the Company made money from textiles, diamonds and so on, the profit was sent to Britain, where a rich minority could build grand houses. Meanwhile in India, millions lost their lands and, in many cases, their lives.

Most of the British in India in the eighteenth century did not benefit directly from the EIC wealth. They remained employed and the number of EIC jobs increased – particularly in the armies – but life for the average Briton in India was often very hard.

High Mortality Rate

Life expectancy in India was certainly lower than back in Britain and there was widespread illness: malaria, cholera, typhoid and the plague were all common. Florence Nightingale wrote: 'But the main causes of disease in India, want of drainage, want of water supply for stations and towns, want of proper barracks and hospitals, remain as before in all their primitive perfection.'[4] Julius Jeffreys wrote: 'The mortality of *barrack-children* is appalling, especially in the months of June, September, and October. At Cawnpore from twenty to thirty have died in one month.'[5]

From perilous sea travel to the unfamiliar climate, poor hygiene and disease, life in and en route to India provided ample opportunity for death. Many eighteenth-century civil servants never returned home and various military conflicts from the eighteenth to twentieth centuries led to high numbers of deaths among British troops based in the area.

Allen's Indian mail, and register of intelligence for British and foreign India, China, and all parts of the East includes the following letter from 'a Field Officer at the Oriental Club':

> Clearly there are more deaths at the Bengal presidency than at Madras and Bombay; but Bombay in 1846 had the greatest number of deaths, Madras in 1848 the fewest. Bengal had more troops employed during the ten years; Bombay had a good proportion of troops engaged; Madras but few troops, and those chiefly in China. There must be some consideration paid to climate. The Madras troops (except those at Saugor and near the Nerbudda) are located to the south of Calcutta. The Bombay troops are stationed in the west of India, and more to the north, generally, than the Madras troops. Cholera should be separately stated. It should be shown whether those who died had been on service or not, for diseases are caused by exposure on service, and do not appear, perhaps, till some time after the campaign is over. The Queen's inspector-general of hospitals told me – alluding to the men who died from the effects of wounds in the Sikh battles, – that it would require months, if not a year, before the number of men could be stated

who died from the effects of wounds: so men not wounded, but employed on service, may die from diseases originating from employment on service, and may be included among the deaths from 'ordinary causes'![6]

Encouragement of marriages to female Indians. From 1770 'there was wholesale interracial sexual exploration and surprisingly widespread cultural assimilation and hybridity ... Virtually all Englishmen in India at this period Indianised themselves to some extent.'[7] Anyone with male British ancestors in India at this period should be open to the possibility of them having married or taken a mistress among the Indian population. As most soldiers of other ranks in the Company's armies were not allowed to marry, many cohabited with native women instead. Some Indians, particularly women, converted to Christianity in this period, and thus may be found among church (ecclesiastical) records (see Chapter 7). However, only a minority of Britons converted to Hinduism or Islam.

In 1791, when the British discovered they were outnumbered in India by 'Eurasians', Cornwallis (see below) introduced laws excluding Eurasians from senior military and civil positions, from moving out of the towns, and from receiving a British education. By the early 1800s it was socially unacceptable for the British to associate with Anglo-Indians. Nevertheless, up to around 1830, several Britons continued to defy the race and culture barrier by wearing Indian dress, smoking hookahs, chewing betel-nut, and speaking Indian languages. In the case of James Achilles Kirkpatrick, the British Resident in Hyderabad from 1798–1805, this included illicitly marrying an Indian princess, Khair-un-Nissa, in a Muslim ceremony. Their marriage ended tragically when Kirkpatrick died only five years later. His children were then sent to their grandfather in England, never to see their mother again. His daughter, Katherine Aurora 'Kitty' Kirkpatrick 'had initially been brought up as Sahib Begum, a Muslim noblewoman in Hyderabad' but received a Christian baptism when she arrived in London. This baptism can be found among the records of St Marylebone parish in London baptisms, marriages and burials on www.ancestry.co.uk or at Westminster City Archives.

Other fathers, such as district collector Richmond Thackeray brought up the children of their *bibi* (female companion) alongside their legitimate children. Richmond's son, William Makepeace Thackeray, later a famous author, was raised alongside his half-sister, Amelia, the daughter of an unknown Indian woman.

Of course, not all the British approved of this hybrid life. Governor Wellesley, for example, was very concerned about the behaviour of Kirkpatrick in 1801, and dismissed him from his post in 1805.

Records in England such as parish registers should not be overlooked when searching for British Indian ancestors. Many ancestors returned to Britain either temporarily or permanently, and may have left a paper trail of activities on these shores. The registers can be found in local and parish record offices, or with the local church. Some registers can also be found on subscription websites like www.ancestry.co.uk, www. findmypast.co.uk or www.thegenealogist.co.uk. Some are also indexed on www.familysearch.org.

One of the best resources for learning about how life in India could appear to those newly-arrived from Georgian Britain is the collection of frank, rambling letters written by the newly-married Eliza Fay, beginning with descriptions of her sea passage to Calcutta in 1779 and her capture by bandits in Egypt. Unlike many of the authors of letters and diaries from this period, Eliza Fay was not well-educated and experienced periods of fairly low social status. Unguarded in their portrayal of all she saw around her, the letters are available to read online at http:// www.archive.org/stream/originalletters00forsgoog#page/n6/mode/2up.

Vital records are sparse in this early period but the following alternatives may help you find birth, marriage or death information for your ancestors.

Records of Britons Resident in India

Early directories
Directories are very useful for telling us about ancestors of all classes, and their very existence illustrates the growth of the printing industry among the European population in India. Many surviving directories can be found on the open shelves in AAS, and include names of residents in eighteenth-century Bengal, Bombay, Madras and St Helena.

The *India Calendar* of the eighteenth century was produced by the Honorable Company's Press and lists EIC servants of all levels, and major European residents in Calcutta. Other useful directories for this period are the *Bengal Kalendar and Register* (Chronicle Press) and the *Civil and Military Register* (the *Indian Gazette* Office). Most of the directories include names of senior civil servants and military officers.

Some directories introduced Birth, Marriage and Death announcements, which are sensible to search if you know roughly when an event occurred but cannot find it in the Ecclesiastical Returns. Another use for these directories is the section on arrivals and departures, both of ships and of notable European residents.

Indian Directories are explored in more detail in Richard Morgan's FIBIS Fact File No. 3 on the subject but the main titles to explore can be found on the British Library's shelves at OIR.354.

Deaths of ancestors can be traced through announcements in directories. Besides the open-access directories in AAS there are similar databases on the FIBIS website, such as transcripts of domestic announcements 1806–67 from the *Bombay Almanac*, which include names, ages and occupations, and of the *East India Register* of 1809–44. Those named include many military and marine officers, several senior civil servants, some wives and children, plus the occasional coachmaker, painter and musician.

Newspapers of this period are also useful. One of the earliest, the weekly *India Gazette*, mentions names of several Europeans who lived in India in the eighteenth century, and could be scurrilous in its accusations in the early years. The very first newspaper in India, *Hicky's Bengal Gazette*, was published in the English language and was founded by a former trader, James Augustus Hicky in 1780.

However, most printers were occupied with advertising, stationery and almanacs. All kinds of pamphlets were created according to the growing needs of the British: calendars (for Muslim, Hindu and Christian years), treatises, vocabulary guides, and maps.

Lists of residents

More information on European inhabitants in Bengal, Madras and Bombay in this early period (1688–1830) can be found in the British Library in reference IOR/O/5/26–31. This includes yearly lists of names in alphabetical order (some indexed), which show the country of origin of each resident, the length of their residence in the Presidency, their occupation and their dwelling. Some of these records have been filmed and are available at LDS family history centres. FIBIS now has data from IOR/O/5/26 & 27 on its website, including:

Bengal Inhabitants 1809
European Inhabitants in Bengal 1805
European Residents in Calcutta Environs 1793
European Residents in *Mofussil* 1793
European Residents of Calcutta 1793
Europeans residing at Madras and its Environs 1800–01

Madras Inhabitants 1811
Madras Inhabitants 1816
Fort St George Inhabitants 1701–07
Madras Inhabitants 1688

Mofussil referred to rural areas bordering the Presidency capitals of Bombay, Calcutta and Madras; later the term was used (sometimes derogatorily) for other rural areas.

Further notes on European residents living in India between 1766 and 1829 are held in reference IOR/O/5/1–25. These notes are taken from government records of both civil and criminal proceedings.

Index Z/O/6/1–2 on the open shelves of AAS relates to names in reference IOR/O/6/1–20. This refers to East India House memoranda 1794–1841 on 'the service and character of individuals, memorials, complaints, claims, petitions, suggestions on administrative charges'.

Notes
1. *Imperial Gazetteer of India*, vol. IV, 1907, p. 46.
2. Ordnance Survey.
3. Kevin P. Phillips, *Wealth and Democracy*.
4. Florence Nightingale, *How People may Live and not Die in India*.
5. Julius Jeffreys, *The British army in India: its preservation by an appropriate clothing, housing [&c.]*.
6. *Allen's Indian mail*, vol. 9, 1851.
7. William Dalrymple, *White Mughals*, p. 10.

Chapter 3

COMPANY RULE IN INDIA

The first step to empire is revolution, by which power is conferred; the next is good laws, good order, good institutions, to give that power stability. I am sorry to say that the reverse of this policy was the principle on which the gentlemen in India acted.

Edmund Burke's Speech on the Impeachment of
Warren Hastings (1788)

Governors of India

As men like Clive gained land, power and riches, corruption spread in the higher echelons of the East India Company. Back in London shareholders became disgruntled, and the British Government realized a need to assert its control over the EIC. In 1773 when its charter was due for renewal, the Company's losses were so great that it was obliged to apply for a loan from the Government. The loan was provided but in order to limit the power and corruption of the EIC, the Regulating Act brought all three Presidencies under a single governor-general who also acted as Governor of the Presidency of Fort William (Bengal) until 1854. This position allowed for supervision of EIC employees in other areas of India by a Council, and was the beginning of the period known as 'Company Rule'.

Warren Hastings (first Governor-General of the Presidency of Fort William from 1773–83)

Along with Clive, Hastings is credited as laying the foundations of the Company's power in Bengal. He had joined the EIC as a Writer when he was aged just 17. After great success in the Civil Service, he settled in India. He spoke Persian and Hindi fluently, took mistresses and wives from the Indian population, and encouraged other EIC employees to marry Indian women and adopt Indian customs. He became Governor of Bengal and then the first Governor-General.

Civil service directories often list the many languages spoken by EIC employees. Men at this time may have married more than once; therefore all records of marriage should be checked, including ecclesiastical returns, directories, and newspaper announcements held in the British Library.

By 1773 when Hastings was ruling India, the EIC army was 100,000-strong; all paid for by taxing the Indian population. The taxes were successfully funding the Industrial Revolution in Britain but had a disastrous effect on the Indian economy: famines in 1783–4 (killing 5 million people in Bengal), followed by further famines at the turn of the century. However, local Indians could still reach high positions of government as Hastings ran a racially cohesive regime.

The British Government and company directors were concerned that territorial expansion was happening too fast and wanted it halted. Unfortunately, politics dictated that in order to protect itself from possible enemies, the EIC needed to forge alliances with neighbouring states. These alliances led to the EIC becoming involved in the expensive Second Anglo-Mysore War (1780–4) in southern India, during which the Madras Presidency nearly collapsed under the assault of 'the Tiger of Mysore', Tipu Sultan in 1782. Tipu Sultan, the de facto ruler of the princely state of Mysore, was an ally of the French and a continual thorn in the side of the EIC from the 1770s onward. The First Anglo-Maratha War (1777–83) saw the Company challenge the Maratha Empire near its base of Poona.

There are several personal papers in the European manuscripts (MSS Eur) series written by Britons who experienced these wars. Even if your ancestors or their regiments are not mentioned, you can use these records to gain some understanding of what life was like for them during this period.

Back in London, William Pitt's government passed the East India Act of 1784 establishing a Board of Control, the president of which was responsible for overseeing the EIC's diplomatic, military and financial concerns from London. The British Government disliked Hastings' adoption of Indian customs and his attempts to restore Indian rules to government of the subcontinent. The increasing debts created by the wars and extended territory were also of real concern. Consequently, charged with mismanagement in 1785, Hastings was recalled to England. On his return in 1786 he was impeached under the Regulating Act, which forbade acceptance of gifts from Indian leaders. Although his trial began in 1788, Hastings was proved innocent only in 1795.

This incident indicated a toughening of British attitudes to immersion in Indian culture. From this point, Britons were discouraged from mixing with the local population. The British Government wanted to 'improve' India in a strict but benevolent manner. They thus began to abandon attempts to rule the country in Indian ways and with Indian rulers.

Charles Cornwallis – 2nd Earl Cornwallis (1786–1795)

Before Wellesley came to power, there was another reforming governor-general whose laws created a greater separation between the British and the local population. Lord Cornwallis was sent to India 'to curtail the rapine [and corruption] and bring Bengal under both British and "civilized" government' (Marshall). He was the first governor-general appointed under the terms of the East India Act. A former soldier, he introduced private property rights in land through a Permanent Settlement of 1793, separated the civil and military powers of state, and established a new legal system. He created a professional civil service where income came from official salaries, no longer from trade or bribes. There were also to be training schools at Haileybury and Fort William College, from where civil servants emerged with a different attitude from their predecessors. Eventually, this led to government by less military-minded men, and thus a less aggressive tendency.

Haileybury College Archives holds records of the former East India College and its pupils – the future civil servants of India. The college trained civil servants between 1806 and 1858. More information can be found on the website http://www.haileybury.com/the-school/a-brief-history/archives.

Cornwallis was infuriated by the decadent behaviour of the ruling British overseas, and believed that the corruption and weak rule were undermining Britain. As a result of Cornwallis's fight against corruption, the nature of British rule was changed for ever. So too were attitudes to Indians within government, the law, and society. Cornwallis believed that Indians were corrupt and that trading with them directly would harm British interests. Consequently, he separated government between the British in senior roles, and Indians in more junior positions.

The British had been distressed by the success of the sultans of Mysore over the EIC's Madras administration. Concerned about the efficacy of the Madras Government and its Army, the soldierly Cornwallis did not hesitate to take command in the latter stages of the Third Anglo-Mysore War (1789–1792) against Tipu Sultan, who had invaded the princely state of Travancore in 1789. Luckily for the EIC, the French Revolution of the same year and the might of the Royal Navy combined to limit France's support for Tipu Sultan during the three-year battle. Severely weakened, Tipu Sultan was forced to cede half of Mysore in 1792, thus furthering the expansion of British India.

From 1792 the EIC broke out of Bengal and established military rule in Mysore (1792; 1799) and the Marathas (1803–5; 1816). Throughout this period several princely states survived, although some of these were effectively under British control.

One of the most significant actions of Cornwallis's rule was his 1793 permanent settlement of Bengal's land revenues. Taxation had been a huge cause of consternation under Hastings, and Cornwallis attempted to create a fair and stable system in order to try to avoid economic problems and famine. He also feared war with France in these revolutionary times and wanted to placate the Bengal landlords.

Cornwallis left India in 1793 to support the allies in their fight against the French, who had declared war on Britain earlier that year. He returned to India a few years later to try to help bring peace to the increasingly troubled land. After falling ill on arrival, he died in 1805 at Ghazipur, near Benares. Cornwallis's correspondence was published in three volumes in 1851 and can be viewed or downloaded from http://www.archive.org/details/correspondencec04corngoog.

After Cornwallis's departure, the British Parliament and the Board of Control took an even firmer hold on India.

Civil Servants

Many Europeans in India in this period were in the employ of the East India Company, either in a military role or as a civil servant. Civil servants ran India on an everyday basis, from dispensing justice to dealing with famines and plagues.

In the early years of the sixteenth and seventeenth centuries, EIC officers were known as Factors – that is, agents for the factories (i.e. warehouses) at the Company's forts. Before becoming a Factor, an agent may have been an Apprentice. As the Company grew, so more senior staff emerged and they were known as Merchants. As the Company's land and power grew, it became more involved in taxation and justice, thus the role of these covenanted civil servants became adapted to administrate the Company's new activities.

Records of the covenants of appointment/articles of agreement for 1771–1946 are found in the British Library reference IOR/O/1. They include the name of the covenanted civil servant, the occupation sought, names of referees, and the amount of salary or bond. An Index of Bombay Civil Servants can be found in reference O/6/32–35.

Later less senior, uncovenanted civil servants, including those who worked in the Indian Police Force, Public Works employees, telegraphers, forestry officials etc., were also employed. Records of them are covered in more detail in the next chapter. All lower-ranking civil servants were recruited in India, often from the Anglo-Indian community or from among retired soldiers. There are details of these civil servants in series L/F/10, giving name, occupation, salary and period of residence in India covering 1818–1900. The index of records contained in L/F/10 can now be found at FIBIwiki: http://www.wiki.fibis.org/index.php?title=Category:L/F/10.

Some of the published directories mentioned above give lists of civil servants, their rank (i.e. Writer, Factor, Junior Merchant, or Senior Merchant) and the year of appointment.

The Bengal, Madras and Bombay Civil funds (closed c1885) provided pensions for the widows and children of civil servants. Details include names of subscribers, their wives, children, and birth and death dates.

Entry Papers: Index of Writers' Petitions. From the end of the seventeenth century, the apprentice civil servants of the EIC were known as Writers. The Writers worked either as copying clerks or bookkeepers. For biographical information on civil servants, see the Index of Writers' Petitions & Committee of College References 1749–1856 (J/1–4 East India College, Haileybury) in AAS. These include baptism certificates, genealogical information and educational testimonials. Sadly, not all papers survive. There is further information on these and other relevant records in Farrington's *The Records of the East India College Haileybury and Other Institutions.* Applications for civil service will be digitized on www.findmypast.co.uk in early 2012.

A typical Writer would earn £10 per annum, and would hope to progress to Factor within three years, when he could earn £20. From then, he should work for three years before becoming a Junior Merchant and then progress to Senior Merchant. The low wages received by Writers often led to many dealing privately in goods in order to make money to send back to Britain. However, the stern Lord Cornwallis abolished this practice officially in 1793.

Richard Colley Wellesley (1798–1805)

As might be expected from the elder brother of the future Duke of Wellington, Wellesley oversaw a more blatant military campaign, fighting to gain control of all the major Indian states. In 1796 the EIC had annexed the Dutch East India Company settlements in Ceylon to the Presidency of Madras (by 1815, the whole of Ceylon was ruled by Britain). From the 1790s onwards, there were fifty years of sporadic wars, including the Fourth Anglo-Mysore War (1798–99) and the Second Anglo-Maratha War (1803–05). It was under Wellesley that the Treaty of Bassein was signed in 1802, signalling the EIC's supremacy in India. In fact Wellesley saw EIC rule expand so far that, exacerbated by heavy military costs, the company's debts tripled. Many Britons enlisted to work for EIC armies or British regiments in India in this period (see Chapter 5).

Growth of the EIC

In 1806, the Company opened the East India Docks in London, which operated as the official import and export dock for Indian cargo until 1967. Inspired by the success of the new West India Docks, the safer moorings of their own docks helped to protect EIC goods from piracy and theft while unloading on the River Thames. The EIC opened an oft-visited Museum and Library in its vast headquarters at East India House in Leadenhall Street in 1801. Although the building was pulled down in 1869 after the company's decline, the Museum artefacts and library papers were safeguarded for the future. Many of the Museum's exhibits are now housed in the Victoria & Albert Museum, the British Museum, the Natural History Museum and Kew Gardens. Most of the surviving contents of the Library became part of the India Office Records, which have been held at the British Library since 1982.

Francis Rawdon-Hastings (1813–23) oversaw the final defeat of the Maratha Confederacy after the Third Anglo-Maratha War (Pindari War) of 1817–18. In 1818 the abdication of the Peshwa of Poona secured the EIC's supremacy, and in 1819 the EIC secured Singapore, where Sir Stamford Raffles established a major trading post.

Around this period, the EIC's military presence became more visible, particularly when collecting taxes or suppressing any form of civil disorder. Floggings and torture were not uncommon. In 1826 an Anglo-Dutch Treaty recognized EIC control of Penang, Singapore and Malacca. This was the foundation of the future colony, the Straits Settlements.

At the end of the 1820s, India's economy suffered a great depression. As Britain's cotton factories boomed and cheap printing of patterns on calicoes in Britain replaced the slower Indian craft of painting chintz, Indian cloth-makers were put out of business and pushed onto the land. With so many new food producers the market was saturated and prices soon fell, once again causing widespread famine among the many agricultural workers.

Life for the British in India

Everyday life in India was still proving a shock to many Britons. For newcomers, experienced at most with a raging bull or frightened horses in the streets, the regular sights of tigers, elephants and dromedary camels could prove terrifying. Nevertheless, tiger- and elephant-hunting were popular sports in India, particularly among the princely classes, and many Britons soon learned to enjoy this. There are several sporting magazines in the British Library's collections, such as the *Bengal Sporting Magazine*, that give an insight into this aspect of British Indian social life and which are useful for discovering sporting, hunting or gambling ancestors. They are not indexed and are difficult to search but it can be rewarding to discover an ancestor in them.

Line drawing of Europeans playing rugby football in Calcutta. (*Illustrated London News*, 1875, from http://commons.wikimedia.org/wiki/Category:British_India)

Contemporary books are also useful. In *The Oriental annual, or, Scenes in India*, William Daniell, Hobart Caunter and Thomas Bacon describe an encounter with tigers in Gingee:

> Tigers are very numerous in this neighbourhood, and some of the natives are remarkably expert in destroying them. During our stay here, for we made a halt of two days, a bullock was killed and taken off by one of these feline plunderers. The print of its foot was to be traced as far as the next village, about six or seven miles from Gingee, where we lost sight of it. Before we left this town, we had a singular evidence of the skill of the natives in destroying the tiger, with which this part of the country is infested.

Elephants were not hunted merely for sport or their tusks. They were also a form of transport.

Not all Britons assimilated well in India, particularly the few British women who were there in this early period. Some aspects of Indian culture were difficult for the British to understand. The reforming Governor-General, William Bentinck (1829–35), legislated against *suttee* (when a widow was burned on her husband's funeral pyre) and female infanticide – both of which had horrified the British ever since they heard of how the founder of Calcutta, Job Charnock, saved the mother of his future children from her husband's funeral pyre in around 1663.

Contact with Britain was slow and many Britons felt cut off from their homeland. The EIC controlled the postal service between Britain and India until 1813 when its monopoly of trade with India was stopped. However, the Company continued to carry mail until 1854, charging nothing for the service. Sadly, much of this post was lost at sea; some of it including records like the Ecclesiastical Returns. This is one reason behind the lack of records or gaps within some series.

Twilight Years of the East India Company

In some ways, the administration was becoming more cohesive and less corrupt. In 1833, the Governor-General's control was extended to all British India, and the official title became the Governor-General of India. Shortly afterwards the EIC's trading monopoly was abolished completely, and there was officially no more opium-trading with China.

However, the borders of British control continued to extend: in 1839, the EIC conquered Aden, and in 1843 the celebrated Major-General Sir Charles Napier defeated the rulers of Sind. From 1844 Governor-General Charles Stewart Hardinge oversaw the Anglo-Sikh War, fighting the Sikh

Empire in the north-west from 1845–6 and 1848–9. These battles, along with the death of the first Maharajah of the Sikh Empire, Ranjit Singh in 1839 resulted in the subjugation of the Sikh Empire, and annexation by the company of the Punjab and (what was later known as) the North-West Frontier Province.

Overall, too much territory had been gained in a short time and the British Government was failing to maintain control. Despite administrative changes and greater control from London, British rule in India in the 1840s was increasingly expensive and chaotic. Anti-British feeling was growing among the local population, particularly as a result of Cornwallis's and Bentinck's unpopular reforms. These reforms also required more British administrators and soldiers to assist in Company rule. For many, work in India provided an exciting opportunity. The EIC had become accustomed to its position in India, and none of the British there in 1850 could have foretold the drama that was to unfold in the forthcoming decade.

Chapter 4

THE INDIA OFFICE AND
THE *RAJ*

*English men and women in India are, as it were, members of one great
family, aliens under one sky.*

Maud Diver, *The Englishwoman in India* (1909)

1857 Indian Mutiny

The year 1857 saw the most radical upheaval for the British in India.
Throughout the 1850s, attitudes among many Indians were hardening
against the British: famines, loss of artisan work, high taxation, and the
use of flogging had only increased the antipathy. Governor-General
Lord Dalhousie, in particular, was unpopular due to his enthusiasm for
Westernization, conversion to evangelical Christianity and his introduction of the annexation of princely states to the East India Company.

The Indian aristocracy (*Rajahs*) and the lower middle-class *sepoys*
(Indian soldiers in the service of the British) were angered further by
their sense of exclusion from the British success that they had helped
to create. No Indian served in the upper echelons of the civil service,
and *sepoys* were prevented from commanding EIC forces, even after
forty years of excellent service. Also support was now growing for the
reinstatement of the Mughal Empire.

All of this laid the tinder for the Indian Mutiny. The spark that set it
aflame was the order to use cartridges for the new Enfield Rifle. The
sepoys refused to bite the tops from these cartridges, as was required,
believing they were oiled with fat from both cows (the holy animal of
Hindus) and pigs (considered offensive to Muslims).

An initial mutiny began among the 19th Bengal Infantry at Berhampur
in late February and among the 34th at Barrackpore in March. As early as
April 1857, *The Times* (London) wrote:

Your Calcutta correspondent may have mentioned the stir among
the high-caste Sepoys at Barrackpore upon learning or fancying that

animal fat was used in the manufacture of some new cartridges, and thus, upon their biting off the end, brought into conduct with their lips.

However, the full fire of the mutiny began on 10 May 1857 in Meerut, near Delhi, after eighty-five men of the 3rd Bengal Light Cavalry were jailed for refusing to use the cartridges. After rescuing their colleagues, the rebels turned their anger on the European *cantonment*, killing women and children. Soon the violence spread into further mutinies in Dinapore, Lucknow, Agra and Umballa.

Shocking scenes followed, many of which were relayed to a horrified public back in Britain. Fear among the British in India reached a peak after several were attacked by their own servants and guards. For many Britons, these events destroyed a sense of trust in the local population. The memories of Katherine Bartrum's (wife of Surgeon Robert Henry Bartrum) terrifying experience of the siege of Lucknow, as well as that of many other Britons, can be found in the European manuscripts in the British Library (MSS Eur/A.69) and in the private papers in the Cambridge South Asian Archive.

These events are also known as India's First War of Independence, the Great Rebellion, the Indian Mutiny, the Revolt of 1857, and the Sepoy Mutiny.

Ultimately, the British military strength (with its forces of mainly Indian troops) was too great and better organized than the rebels. Delhi, the former Mughal capital, was recaptured in September 1857, and Lucknow (which had been abandoned in November 1857) was retaken in March 1858. To the horror of the Indian population, the British then took their revenge, destroying villages with what was termed 'The Devil's Wind'.

James St Clair Burns. For his actions in the Mutiny, James St Clair Burns received the Indian Mutiny Medal. The Medal Roll is indexed on the FIBIS website and in *Indian Mutiny Medal Roll 1857–1859*, (British Forces 1998). The entry for James St Clair Burns reads as follows:

No.	Rank	Surname	Christian Name	Unit	Clasp	Remarks
3295	Orderly Room Clerk	Burns	James St Clair	61 F	D	Died 26 March 1858

D = Delhi Clasp 30 May–14 September 1857 (the Siege of Delhi)
61 F = 61st Foot (South Gloucestershire)

Further information on all Britons involved in these events can be found via the Mutiny indexes held in AAS, reference Z/B/94–96 (Military Affairs/Mutiny B/234–236).

The *Raj* and the India Office Records

After the Mutiny, the EIC was dissolved and the last Mughal ruler was exiled to Burma. This heralded the period in British India known as the *Raj* (Hindi for 'rule'). Under the 1858 Government of India Act, direct control of government was transferred to the British Crown and run, in London, by the Secretary of State for India along with the Council of India (whose fifteen members were each required to have spent at least ten years in the country). The documents created by the EIC were now administered by the newly-established India Office.

In India, leadership of the government remained with the Governor-General, now known as the Viceroy: the Queen's representative.

Indian princes and large landholders were rewarded for not joining the rebellion by recognition in state treaties. The British felt it expedient that more Indians be appointed to the senior levels of ICS (Indian Civil Service). However, those posted to the Legislative tended to be from privileged backgrounds and were largely sympathetic to British interests.

The government halted intervention into Indian social and religious customs, and completely reconstructed the armed forces to prevent any repeat of the recent mutiny.

Queen Victoria was officially proclaimed Empress of India on 1 January 1877, highlighting India's importance to the British Empire.

The Mutiny was never forgotten among Britons, as illustrated by their strong opposition in both Britain and India to the 1883 Ilbert Bill. This proposed that Indian judges and magistrates (in District courts) could try British offenders. Tea and indigo planters in particular were concerned that Indian judges would not be impartial but would remember their mistreatment of Indian workers. Memories of the rape of British women by Indian *sepoys* in the Mutiny contributed to fears of British women being humiliated before Indian judges in rape cases.

In 1911 the national capital was transferred from Calcutta to New Delhi. Limited measures of representative government at the provincial level were introduced in 1919 and extended in 1935 but British India remained non-self-governing until 1947.

In 1920 the Indian High Commission was established in London. This took over some of the India Office's roles, including stores, civil leave, pay and pensions, civilian steamship passages and (from 1924) some recruitment for official posts in India.

Civil Service records in the Raj period

A senior position in the ICS was highly sought-after, both in India and at home. Senior members of the ICS were known reverentially as the 'Heaven-born': a term which saw them in a similar light to the highest Hindu caste, the Brahmins. The ICS was praised long after the British left for being incorruptible and its efficiency was seen as a great legacy of British India.

Sources for recruitment into the Indian Civil Service 1855–1946 are detailed in Baxter's Guide, *Biographical Sources in the India Office Records* (third edition, 2004). There are also brief biographies in the form of lists of appointments for senior civil servants 1886–1947 in the *India List* and, from 1907, the *India Office List* in AAS (OIR.354.54). Baxter's Guide gives details of sources on recruitment to the Indian Civil Service 1855–1946. *Histories of Service* in series V/12 gives details of promotions and posting and sometimes dates of birth for high-ranking officers from 1879. The annual Civil Lists from 1840 in series V/13 give information on the careers of middle- and high-ranking officials for each year. The full series thus needs to be checked to learn about the complete career. Promotion was given for length of service. Members of the judiciary can also be found in the V/12 records.

The Bengal Civil Service graduation list for 1869 can be viewed on www.findmypast.co.uk and further details on this can be found on the FIBIS database.

Changes in Social Life

In India

After the Mutiny, the expatriate community retreated into itself, socializing among itself:

> It was still the custom for the English to take the air in the evening in [Calcutta's] Eden Gardens, perhaps to listen to the music of a regimental band, but mainly to see and be seen. In the cool weather when the Viceroy was in residence and the Calcutta season in full swing, there were balls and dances almost every night.[1]

Hunting and sport remained popular, and in 1862 British officers Captain Robert Stewart and Major-General Joe Shearer founded the first polo club at Calcutta (the game of polo having originated in India).

Life for British Indians was often ruled by the weather. The British in the capital, Calcutta and eastern Bengal would be fearful of embarking on the seas in the cyclone month of October. The weather became increasingly warm from April until the August rains, which tailed off during the humid season of September and October. From 1864 during the hottest season the Viceroy and the elite of British in India moved to Simla, the summer capital.

Less elite Britons would escape the heat of the cities and plains by relocating to the cooler hill stations. The roads to the hill stations were built by the Army as they marched up to 25 miles per day and were located near to the chief areas of British settlement. British administrators moved the business of each Presidency for the summer, despite the awkwardness of doing this. Darjeeling had been the informal summer capital for the Bengal Presidency since 1840. Ootacamund – known as Ooty – in the Nilgiri hills was the summer base for the Madras Presidency and known as 'snooty Ooty' for the period when the Governor was in residence; and Mahabaleshwar was the retreat for Bombay. The Governor of Uttar Pradesh and members of the Lucknow secretariat travelled over 200 miles to Naini Tal (Nainital). Other well-known hill stations were Mussoorie and Murree.

Dennis Kincaid writes of escaping the heats:

> After the rains it grew hot again in Poona for a few weeks. It would be necessary to run up to Mahabaleshwar where, in October, the wild flowers were at their loveliest and the air fresh and delightful after the monsoon. But it was in May that Mahabaleshwar was most crowded; for then Poona was almost unbearably hot and it was difficult to play games or take any exercise in comfort, while in Mahabaleshwar one could play golf all day.[2]

In the later nineteenth century some improvement was made with illness but poor sanitation remained a problem. Bengal Pilot M.H. Beattie wrote of his time in 1878 Calcutta that cholera, smallpox and plague were 'endemic', probably due to the fact that

> there was no proper drainage system in the town, and much of the scavenging was effected by jackals, vultures, adjutants, crows and pariah dogs. The drains were open and inhabited by bandicoots, enormous rats of whose ferocity old residents gave blood-curdling accounts.[3]

Although there were many deaths from plague even in the early 1900s, progress was made with malaria when Sir Ronald Ross of the Presidency

Wardley family boat trip to Pachmari Hill Station, 1927. (personal collection of Valmay Young)

General Hospital, Calcutta proved that the disease was transmitted by mosquitoes. A mass vaccination programme also dramatically cut deaths from smallpox. However, even in the mid-twentieth century it was said that one could see a man at breakfast and he could be dead by nightfall, so swiftly and so fiercely could the illnesses of India strike.

More information on the medical history of British India after 1857 can be found in the National Library of Scotland's collection in Edinburgh or at http://digital.nls.uk/indiapapers/index.html.

For the children of the *Raj*, however, it was more difficult to be socially segregated. With their days spent in the company of their *ayahs* (and often gardeners, cooks and other domestics), children learned local languages and cultural habits. (See over the photograph of Betty and Val Wardley, who were fluent in Hindi and Urdu.) Rudyard Kipling, who was born in Bombay in 1865, remembered:

> In the afternoon heats before we took our sleep, she [the Portuguese *ayah*, or nanny] or Meeta [the Hindu bearer, or male attendant] would tell us stories and Indian nursery songs all unforgotten, and we were sent into the dining-room after we had been dressed, with the caution 'Speak English now to Papa and Mamma.' So one spoke

47

Betty and Val Wardley with their ayah *in Jubbulpore, 1927.* (personal collection of Valmay Young)

'English', haltingly translated out of the vernacular idiom that one thought and dreamed in …[4]

Although the British often persisted with the tradition of tea at 4pm and roast meats, they did eat curry and Anglo-Indian creations such as kedgeree or Mulligatawny (traditionally served on Sundays). *The English-woman in India: information for ladies on their outfit, furniture [&c.] by a lady resident* recommended the following for one family dinner:

Hare Soup.
Roast Kid and Mint Sauce.
Mutton Pudding.
Sardine Curry.

The British often combined traditional English fare with ingredients available in their new home. Of available food, the Lady Resident wrote:

Meat is very inferior in size, weight, and goodness to what it is at home; a hind-quarter of mutton weighing from 6 to 10 lbs.
Eggs are so much smaller …
English bacon is extremely expensive …

Tea-planter George Barker wrote in 1884 of how he longed for more variety in the meals served at his planter's bungalow in Assam:

Day succeeds day, and the monotony of chicken meat remains unchanged: chicken in every form, chicken cutlets, steaks, minced, spatch cocked, rissoled, roasted, boiled, curried, in soup, on toast, fried, devilled, and many other ways. No man exists who has been in India and has not been compelled to sit down every day of his life to at least one meal in which chicken figures conspicuously in some form or another.[5]

For many, especially those born there, India was the only home they knew. By 1931, according to Niall Ferguson's *Empire*, there were 168,000 British in India: 60,000 in the Army and police, 4,000 in civil government and 60,000 employed in the private sector.

The Anglo-Indian Community

One of the most significant changes in attitude from the early years of British settlement in India was found with regard to Anglo-Indians. Marriages between British men and local women had become fewer since 1791. After this, British girls were encouraged to travel to India to become wives to British men; marriages among the British community in India were socially approved. After the overland route through Egypt was established in the 1830s, numbers of British women going out to India increased, ushering in the rule of the *memsahib*. This led to a change in morality: there was no longer a culture of heavy drinking and sexual freedom.

After the Great War, the insularity of the British increased as improved communication, assisted passages and the beginning of commercial airlines brought Europe closer. Consequently, Anglo-Indians began to be marginalized and sometimes socially segregated, belonging neither to one community nor the other. Marriages thus began to take place between Anglo-Indians. They were discriminated against in employment also: while Anglo-Indians were sought by employers in areas such as the railways, the forestry service, customs and excise, the Post Office and telegraphs, and in teaching, they tended to be excluded from the higher echelons of public service and military power. Their position in society began to change in the twentieth century as more Indians were employed in these lower-ranking positions instead. Anglo-Indians were required to travel thousands, if not hundreds of thousands of miles for work. Much of this was to be in railway colonies, such as that at Kharagpur. Anglo-Indian women were more likely to be employed in domestic service, teaching hospital nursing or as shorthand typists.

The social snobbery that existed in British India in this period can be difficult to comprehend: one stayer-on in Hugh Purcell's *After The Raj* described it as 'silly'. The class-ridden nature of India and Britain then is evident in how Anglo-Indians were isolated but the maharajahs and Indian members of the ICS were accepted into British society. There were other social rules: members of the ICS, for example, were superior to businessmen, and within business circles, those who worked with tea were superior to those who dealt in jute.

Anglo-Indians even had their own slang or patois, known as *hobson-jobson*, using words from Urdu and English: *box-wallah* (a derogatory term for a European businessman), *bungalow* (country house), *grass widow* (wife at hill station while husband worked in the plains), *jungle-wallah* (forest officer), *memsahib* (lady), *sahib* (Sir), and *Station* (where the district officers lived).

Irene Edwards (née Green) was one of more than sixty survivors of the British *Raj* who were interviewed by the BBC in 1973. These interviews can be found at the British Library in series MSS Eur T.29, or read in Charles Allen's *Plain Tales from the Raj*. Irene was born in 1906 to a railway officer and his wife. She later worked as a nurse, married in

1938 and left India in 1950. Irene told of the colour prejudice and discrimination against Anglo-Indians:

> I knew an Anglo-Indian girl in Peshawar, white with blue eyes, who was known to be Anglo-Indian because her parents lived in Peshawar. She knew I used to go to the club because I used to talk about the parties there and she wanted to join. I asked a lady doctor who had influence to try and get Celia in and she told me it was no use trying 'because everybody round here knows Celia is an Anglo-Indian'. I told this lady doctor, 'Well, so am I.' 'Yes, but people don't know it here. You have passed in the crowd, but Celia won't.'[6]

The club was central to British social life in India, and each civil and military station tended to have one. Most members were from the upper echelons of society, like officers. Lists of clubs can be found in *Thacker's*.

In 1876 the Eurasian and Anglo-India Association (later Anglo-Indian and Domiciled European Association) was established in Bengal. The archived journals of this association may be useful to those with Anglo-Indian ancestors. The present form of this is the All-India Anglo-Indian Association, based in New Delhi; there are roughly sixty-two branches all over India, many of which produce their own newsletters. The most comprehensive site for Anglo-Indian networking is probably http://www.anglo-indians.com, although there is an Anglo-Indian Heritage Centre in Australia, http://www.collectionsaustralia.net/org/1809/about. In 1879 the Anglo-Indian and Domiciled European Association of Southern India (Madras/Chennai) was founded. Around 1900 there was an Imperial Anglo-Indian Association, which re-emerged some years later as the Anglo-Indian Empire League.

Further information can be found in FIBIS Fact File No. 1: *Researching Anglo-Indian ancestry* by Geraldine Charles.

New Occupations and Their Resources

In the 1860s many Britons left for India to work as tea- or coffee-planters (see Chapter 6), to establish cotton mills, or to work on the new railways (see Chapter 7). Engineering and journalism also prospered in this period.

Rudyard Kipling was sent to England for schooling to avoid being 'country bred' (raised in India) which would have prevented him rising to a senior level in many occupations. Many children were sent away as young as 5, often to avoid the danger of the heat. One of these children, Maud Diver, wrote 'One after one England claims them, till the mother's heart and house are left to her desolate.'[7] When Kipling returned to Bombay in 1882, he worked as a journalist. He wrote that once settled, 'my English years fell away, nor ever, I think, came back in full strength'.[8] As for many Britons, India was his true home.

In this period, roles for uncovenanted civil servants grew (see p. 37). Records on personnel employed in railways (e.g. engineers), police, public works, Post Office, etc. are available in AAS for 1818–1900 in IOR/L/F/10 and for 1922–8 in IOR/L/F/10. They include names, occupations, salaries and periods of residence in India. You can trace the careers of some uncovenanted civil servants through the annual Civil Lists of the Public Works Department in V/13. More details can be found in FIBIS Fact File No. 8 by Lawrie Butler. Further information on railway employees can be found in Chapter 8.

At shelf-mark IOR LISTS L/AG/34/14 there is also a list of Deaths of Uncovenanted Civil Servants and Other Officers 1870–1947, including names of the deceased, dates and places of deaths, ranks, sometimes age, native town and country, next-of-kin, and custody of property if any.

Where no entry for a family can be found in *Thacker's* (see below), it is worth checking library catalogues for local directories, such as the *Guide to Poona, 1902*. These are more likely to include the names of less notable residents, and may also feature images of the area and contemporary maps. Private papers for those who worked in the Police and Forestry Services can be found in the Cambridge South Asian Archive.

Later Directories

With the introduction of the *Raj* came the unification of directories like the *Indian Civil List* into one large volume with an index combining information and residents from all the three Presidencies. *Thacker's Indian Directory* is similarly combined. This ran from 1885–1960, and for Bengal only as *Thacker's Bengal Directory* from 1864–84. The most useful part of these for family history is the index to European residents. However, not many lower-status Europeans were included.

Aside from alphabetical lists of residents, *Thacker's* also includes details useful for understanding your ancestors' lives in India. There is information on where to send a telegram, of the Post Offices, schools, churches, missions, charities and hospitals. Official lists include members of the government, military and civil officers; and addresses and senior officers of the forest, telegraph, postal, survey and police departments. The maps of railways and the city of Calcutta help to plot India's ever-changing vastness. More unusual are the addresses for *Dak bungalows,*

Gustav Kuhlmey, Bandmaster and Musical Director. (personal collection of Valmay Young)

the government guest houses in remote areas where the British would often stay en route to a hill station, or while undertaking government work, hunting or trekking.

Freemason ancestors and details of their Lodges can be traced through directories. Further information is found on FIBIwiki, including titles of Masonic histories available online. Membership records, annual returns and available correspondence between Lodges in Britain and India are held at the Library and Museum of Freemasonry, 60 Great Queen Street, London. A Genealogical Request Form can be sent via the website at http://www.freemasonry.london.museum/family-history.

The rich variety of merchants and the types of products available within India and for export is shown through the trade section. Among these products were tea, coffee, cotton, cloth, indigo, soap, jute, betel-nut, mustard, lime, timber, tobacco, India rubber, teak, ivory, pepper, arsenic, gold, spices and salt.

All of the directories cited here (unless other archive mentioned) can be found in the British Library. Do bear in mind that the publisher would have included details given to them which may or may not be accurate, therefore you may find an ancestor in a directory in a year in which they were no longer alive.

Some unofficial directories continued in the Presidencies. In Madras from 1862–1936 there was the *Asylum Press Almanac* (previously the *Madras Almanac, Madras Register*), which is particularly useful regarding specific trades, societies, hospitals and councils in the area.

The original *Bombay Kalendar and Register* (from 1806) became the *Bombay Almanac and Directory* but only up to 1868. The *Times of India Calendar & Directory* (Bombay Directory) ran until around 1930.

In Bengal the latest directory, *The New Calcutta Directory*, only ran until 1862.

Coverage for Ceylon is more patchy: the British Library holds the *Ceylon Almanac and Annual Register* in its various forms for some years between 1851 and 1888, while SOG has the more recent *Ferguson's Ceylon Directory* for 1863, 1903–4, 1926 and 1940. Experiences of those who lived in Ceylon can be found among the private papers at the Cambridge South Asian Archive.

Growth of Empire: Expansion into Africa

In 1869 the Suez Canal was opened. This enabled the British to travel to and from India without having to go round the Cape. Travel to India now took considerably less time and, together with the telegraph lines between India and Britain (connected in 1870), Britain felt nearer to those away from home.

In the search for the source of the River Nile (and to ensure its waters continued to flow through the arid lands of Egypt), Britain occupied Nigeria, Kenya and Uganda. Without India, it is arguable whether Britain would have extended its empire to Africa at all. The continent was dangerous country, and much exploratory and missionary activity up to this point had led to early deaths and little territorial gain.

The Cape Colony had been taken from the Dutch East India Company in 1795 to ensure the safety of British ships en route to India. In the 1870s Britain began to expand beyond that into the Transvaal and the colonies of South Africa. By 1880, Britain held Freetown in Sierra Leone, forts along the Gambian coast, the Gold Coast protectorate and held a presence in Lagos.

In 1875 Britain became a minority (44 per cent) shareholder in the Suez Company, and was determined to maintain control of the canal, through war and peace, after seizing power on 25 August 1882. From here, Britain began her occupation of Egypt (formally declared a protectorate in 1914) and then Sudan.

This New Imperialist period has become known as the Scramble for Africa (1880–1900), as European powers raced to occupy the continent. This imperialism was formalized via the General Act of the Conference of Berlin in 1885. The wealth that paid for Britain's exploration, the materials that help to manufacture weapons and feed troops, came largely from India.

Viceroys

The first Viceroy appointed after the Mutiny was Earl 'Clemency' Canning (1858–62), who had been Governor-General since February 1856. Under his fairly liberal governance, formal direct rule was implemented in India. Information on Canning's Indian Papers is available at http://www.microform.co.uk/guides/R50039.pdf.

Sir John Laird Lawrence (1864–9) improved health and sanitation, encouraged self-government (notably in Bengal 1864) and oversaw the growth of the railway system. The Earl of Mayo (1869–72) continued the work on the railways and also encouraged irrigation and forestry.

Edward Bulwer-Lytton ruled during the Great Famine of 1876–8 (see image) which resulted in the deaths of millions. Lytton's policy of abolishing duty on cotton is held responsible for the terrible extent of the famine, due to the detrimental effect it had on India's cotton industry. In contrast back home, English textile mills flourished. He also introduced income tax. Lytton resigned as a result of criticism over his handling of the famine but not until he had opened the civil service to all in India in 1879.

In 1898, George Nathaniel Curzon arrived in India to take up the post of Viceroy. This was the achievement of a lifetime ambition for Curzon, who had spent 1877–95 travelling around Asia in preparation for what he felt to be his destiny. Among his many initiatives he established the new province of the North-West Frontier and began restoration work on the Taj Mahal. More controversially he held commissions on areas of Indian administration, such as education and policing, and partitioned Bengal (revoked in 1912). His despotic handling of the Indian Civil Service angered those who worked under him, and he refused to sanction the appointment of Indians.

By the time Curzon became Viceroy in this *High Raj* period, the post was regarded as inferior only to that of the Queen and the Prime Minister. The Viceroy and his family were treated like royalty, and indulged in grandeur: the Viceroy's special train, for example, allowed him and his wife a carriage each. Curzon had electric lights and fans

Line drawing of 'The Famine in India: Natives Waiting for Relief at Bangalore' – the Great Famine of 1876–78. (Wikimedia Commons – from the *Illustrated London News*, Saturday 20 October, 1877)

installed in the grand Government House of Calcutta. In the heats the party moved to Simla, where the magnificent Viceregal Lodge had been built in 1888. Their ostentatious life with its 400 servants, gun salutes, grand uniforms, painted elephants, and personal bodyguards was far removed from that of the rest of the Indian and British Indian population outside. His American wife, however, like many wives of the *Raj*, struggled with the heat, illness and frequent separations from her husband (she died from a heart attack in 1906). Curzon began two terms as Governor-General (the second from 1904) but resigned in 1905 after a disagreement with Lord Kitchener (Commander-in-Chief in India). He is also accused of failing to properly control the 1899–1900 famine that killed millions.

Viceroy Gilbert Elliot-Murray-Kynynmound, 4th Earl of Minto, worked with John Morely, the Secretary of State for India, towards the Indian Councils Act of 1909. This is better known as the Morely-Minto reforms, which were intended to curb pleas for nationalism and to reduce the terrorism in Bengal that had begun after Curzon's partition. In order to induce loyalty among the more western and upper-class Indians, the reforms led to Indians being elected to legislative councils and Muslims being given the right of a separate electorate. Previously Indians had only been appointed to official positions, never elected. Although this laid the foundations for the eventual parliamentary system of India, it did not achieve the Indian National Congress's intention of planning for India to become a self-governing colony.

Viceroy Charles Hardinge was the son of a former Governor-General of India. During his reign, George V visited India. Hardinge helped to appease the nationalists, although he was the target of a bomb in 1912. His wife, Winifred, helped to further the medical training of Indian women. Hardinge's efforts resulted in India committing many troops to the First World War but his successor, Frederic Thesiger (Viscount Chelmsford), was less successful in appeasing the nationalists. The Government of India Act 1919 did not extend representation among Indians as far as was wished. Chelmsford reacted badly to the consequent civil unrest, and the Rowlatt Act of 1919 established martial law in some areas. See Chapter 10 for further details of the national movement.

The Amritsar Massacre and the Rise of Indian Nationalism

In April 1919, the Amritsar Massacre took place in the Jallianwala Bagh of Amritsar in the Punjab, an area of some of the worst anti-British protests. In the days leading up to the massacre protests had taken place in the city, and attempts were made to quell them by the military, which shot at the crowd, killing some. In retaliation, protesters attacked banks, government buildings and the railway station. Several Europeans were killed. Even after this protest fell quiet, others took place across the province and three Europeans were murdered. The British Government thus implemented the new martial rule on most of the Punjab. Significantly, this forbade freedom of assembly for groups of more than four.

On 13 April more than 5,000 Sikhs, Hindus and Muslims gathered in the Jallianwala Bagh to celebrate the Sikh festival of Baisakhi. However, others used this opportunity to conduct a political meeting. Some time after the meeting began, Brigadier-General Dyer entered the garden with ninety soldiers, fifty of whom were armed. Without warning, Dyer ordered his men to open fire on the densest section of the crowd. The people could escape only through a few narrow entrances and many of those who escaped the bullets were crushed in the following stampede. The wounded, untended, were left to die by Dyer.

Later the British declared the number killed was 379 but it is believed that the true figure is closer to 1,000. Although officials tried to repress details of the massacre with information only reaching Britain in December 1919, word of the incident spread throughout India spurring further nationalist protests. These protests continued to make life difficult for many British Indian ancestors until partition in 1947.

Burma

The reforming Lord Linlithgow became Viceroy in 1936, having previously overseen the India Act of 1935. During his reign the first general elections were held in all the provinces. He also enabled constitutional changes: Sind became a separate province from Bombay, and Orissa became a new province.

Burma became a separate country with its own constitution, resulting in separate directories and administration. The records of the Burma Office (1937–48) are held within the IOR. They can be found in AAS but are indexed in separate files. The following website may be useful for locating ancestors in this specific area: http://www.angloburmeselibrary. com/index.html. Memories and experiences of those who worked in Burma can be found in the Cambridge South Asian Archive.

Notes
1. Sears, 'The Horizon History of the British Empire' in *Time-Life*, 1973.
2. Dennis Kincaid, *British Social Life in India, 1608–1937*.

3. M.H. Beattie, *On the Hooghly*, p. 202.
4. Rudyard Kipling, *Something of myself and other autographical writings.*
5. George Barker, *A Tea Planter's life in Assam.*
6. Charles Allen, *Plain Tales from the Raj*, p. 140.
7. Maud Diver, *The Englishwoman in India*, 1909.
8. Kipling, ibid.

Chapter 5

THE EAST INDIA COMPANY'S ARMIES, THE INDIAN ARMY, THE BRITISH ARMY IN INDIA AND THE ROYAL INDIAN AIR FORCE

'But what,' said they, 'is a prince without an army? and why do you keep up yours now that all your enemies have been subdued?' 'We want them,' replied Godby, 'to prevent our friends from cutting each other's throats, and to defend them all against a foreign enemy.'

Rambles and Recollections of an Indian Official,
William Sleeman 1788–1856

In the history of British India, more Britons worked in the armed forces than in any other occupation. Some military ancestors lived in India for decades, whereas others were only posted there with the British Army for a short period. Many Britons who served in the lower ranks chose to stay in India, although their descendants may have chosen an alternative career such as on the railways. This chapter covers the armies and the air forces that were based in India but naval ancestors are explored in more detail in the following chapter.

Military activity, particularly the many wars which dominated Britain's early years in India, led to high numbers of Britons from both the Indian and British armies dying and being buried there. As a result, military ancestors can be found in death records, as well as in records created solely for military purposes. Your ancestor may also have been born or married in India, and his children may have been born there. Consequently, even if he was born outside India, he could be traced

60

through copies of his children's baptisms in the IOR. It is therefore worth looking for all siblings in your baptism searches, not just for your immediate ancestor.

All the records listed here should provide further clues for researching your military ancestor in other sources. Some of the clues to look out for include the names of the regiment(s) in which he served: if the regiment is followed by 'N.I.' this stands for 'Native Infantry' and tells you that your ancestor served in one of the units of the EIC armies, which comprised *sepoys* and European commissioned and non-commissioned officers. You can then research further into the activities and locations of his regiment through published histories. Further information on EIC regiments for the three Presidencies can be found by following the respective link at http://wiki.fibis.org/index.php?title=Presidency_Armies. If he served in India with a British Army regiment, a useful website for identifying these regiments is http://www.army.mod.uk/infantry/regiments/default.aspx but do be aware that regiments often changed their name over time. A 'succession of titles' can be found on the website for the Army Museums Ogilvy Trust: www.armymuseums.org.uk. This site can also provide contact details for existing regimental museums. It is important to check that the British Army regiment you are investigating was in India at the time your ancestor was there. Regiments' whereabouts can be traced through the annual *Army Lists* for the British Army from 1798 and in some Indian directories.

All records of the Indian Office's Military Department and the earlier EIC military records are held by the British Library and are in the L/MIL series. This series includes service records of officers and some soldiers, as well as records of military policy, battalion rolls, soldiers' letters, defence schemes, organization of the military, and details of medals and prizes. More detail on these, as well as recruitment lists and embarkation papers for other ranks, can be found in Peter Bailey's *Researching Ancestors in the East India Company Armies* and I.A. Baxter's *India Office Library and Records: A Brief Guide to Biographical Sources*, both available in AAS (IOR LISTS 101b). More detail on this topic can be found in the *Guide to the Records of the India Office Military Department* by A. Farrington.

There is also a detailed index to subjects covered in L/MIL/7/1–19656 (1850–1950) in AAS and online on A2A. Although this index does not include names, the details provide a useful background to your ancestors' military experiences. Applications for military service and details of pension payments to individuals are being digitized on www.findmypast.co.uk.

British Army records up to 1920 are held at TNA and have been digitized on www.findmypast.co.uk and (for those who served in the First World War) www.ancestry.co.uk.

The East India Company's Armies

The East India Company divided its operations into the three Presidency armies of Bengal, Madras and Bombay and it therefore also maintained three armies, each having a number of both European and 'native' regiments, although all regiments were commanded by British officers. These three armies were extremely active in the early years, waging wars across India and beyond. From the 1820s the government of India maintained sixteen European regiments of the line as well as a permanent standing army of 170 *sepoy* regiments, totalling 235,000 men.

Generally, all EIC officer entry and soldier enlistment records are in IOR/L/MIL/9; Bengal Army records are to be found in L/MIL/10; Madras Army in L/MIL/11 and Bombay Army in L/MIL/12.

Service records for EIC European officers and soldiers are held in AAS. Printed books, such as the *East India Register & Army List* (1844–60) and the *Indian Army List* may also be consulted.

OFFICERS

Cadet papers
The chief biographical source for officers of the EIC's armies is the series of entry papers for officer cadets for the period 1789–1860 in L/MIL/9/107–269. Usually officers were appointed in the UK after being nominated by one of the EIC Directors (and from 1784 also by the Board of Control). However, officers appointed in India in the late eighteenth century ('country cadets') were not nominated in the same way and their names are rarely found among these entry papers. From 1809 many EIC officer cadets were trained in Britain at Addiscombe Seminary, near Croydon. Evidence of attendance will be found in the cadet papers.

An Index of Applications Papers for Officer Cadets and Bengal, Madras and Bombay from 1765–1859 is held in AAS (IOR LISTS 209a), and online indexes can be searched via A2A or at http://www.ans.com.au/~rampais/genelogy/india/indexes/cadfram.htm.

There are also Registers of Cadets (L/MIL/9/255–269) dating from 1775, which are useful for researching ancestors whose cadet application papers do not survive or which contain limited information. Before 1775 you should be able to find your officer ancestor in the B series (Minutes of the Court of Directors) and series E/4 (the indexed Company Despatches to India).

Army Lists

Army Lists provide details of regiments with names of commanding and other officers. The *India List* and the *Indian Army List* include names of officers from the EIC Armies, the Indian Army, and of British regiments stationed in India.

Copies of the *East India Register and Army List* (1844–60) held in the British Library give details of officers, and of each regiment by number and current station. The List includes irregular regiments but not regiments of volunteers. Each Presidency had its own army list and there is an index to names in the Bengal, Madras and Bombay Service Army Lists 1753–1859 on open access in AAS.

Hart's Army List and the later British *Army List* may also give details of officers in armies in India. Many copies of the above Army Lists can be found at the British Library and TNA. Others may be found on Google Books or www.archive.org.

Hodson's index

The National Army Museum holds the original Hodson's index: a card index of British officers in the Indian (Imperial) Army, the Bengal Army and the East India Company Army. The index is also available in book form on the open shelves of APAC as *List of the Officers of the Bengal Army 1758–1834*. Entries are very detailed and include a full career outline, baptism and marriage and death details, names of fathers and wives, battles fought, medals awarded, and leave taken.

Jarrard Edward Strickland, officer in the Bombay Army. Jarrard Edward Strickland was born in Kendal, Westmorland in 1782. He enlisted as an officer with the Bombay Army in 1801. After serving with General Lake's force, Strickland was sent home with despatches around 1808. He was captured en route by a French privateer and landed at Algoa Bay (now Port Elizabeth, South Africa). His cadet papers in IOR/L/MIL/9/111/ 563–5 state that he was born at Sizergh on 24 February 1782 and include his signature and an extract from the Family Register of Baptisms at Sizergh, giving his time of birth, godparents' names, and the name of his mother, Cecilia Strickland. A second page tells us his late father's name was Jarrard Strickland. Further information was gained from the

Portrait of J.E. Strickland soon after his return from service as an officer in the Bombay Army. (reproduced by kind permission of the National Trust)

table in Miles & Dodwell's *List of officers of the Indian Army from 1760 to 1834*: a Cadet in 1800 [incorrect entry given], Ensign 22nd May 1801 and Lieutenancy 2nd January 1803. It also states that Strickland was struck off in September 1813 along with two fellow officers; this may have been due to absence from India for more than five years. He was certainly absent between 1810 and 1812 as he was conducting his nephew around Greece and Malta (Standish Papers in Wigan Archives Service: D/D St./ BundleC19/18, 11 Jan 1812). The Cadet Registers in IOR/L/MIL/9/257/ 102v–03 tell us that he was appointed on 7 April 1801 when he was 19 years old (cadets had to be aged between 15 and 22). He served with the Bombay Infantry No 385 (number of certificate); he passed the Committee on 7 April; the EIC director was (John) Manship; (W.) Farrer recommended Strickland to Manship.

OTHER RANKS

The soldiers recruited by the EIC in Great Britain and Ireland were gunners or privates for the artillery and infantry units only. Troopers for

Unidentified Soldier. (personal
collection of Valmay Young)

cavalry units in India were raised from Europe only for a short period
during the 1857 Rebellion.

Embarkation Lists, Registers of Recruits & Depot Registers

Ordinary soldiers are usually identified through musters and other
records by their year of arrival and the name of the ship on which they
embarked to India. Thus some of the best sources of information on
NCOs and ordinary soldiers are the Embarkation Lists 1753–1861 in
L/MIL/9/85–106 (some date from 1740), which list names of recruits,
their places of origin, former occupation, and some names of accompanying wives and children.

There are also Registers of Recruits, and Depot Registers showing
recruits (1801–60) in L/MIL/9/29–46. The Registers of Recruits can be
helpful in providing the parish of birth. However, your ancestor may not
be listed as formal lists of recruits were not begun in all areas of the UK
at the same date: those for Bristol, Newry and Cork, for example, only
date from 1846. Depot Registers are similar to those of recruits but some
date from 1801 and thus may contain ancestors not found in those
registers.

Embarkation lists and other lists of soldiers for Madras can be found in L/MIL/11/104: the Registers of Madras Army European Soldiers 1840–50 (indexed). The East India Company's Army soldiers' embarkation lists in the L/MIL series record the names of ordinary soldiers who embarked in the stated years: ref. L/MIL/9/98 covers Jan 1810–Feb 1816 and ref. L/MIL/9/99 covers Mar 1816–Jun 1824.

Muster Rolls and Casualty Returns

Further information on soldiers' service can be found by tracing their careers and their battalions through the Annual Muster Rolls and Casualty Returns (1708–1865) in L/MIL/10, 11 and 12. The Muster Rolls are particularly worth checking for the end of your ancestor's service as they name Pensioners who remained in India, and whose service records may not survive. The deaths of these Pensioners can be found in 'Casualties by Death'.

Also in these series are registers of EIC European soldiers (L/MIL/11), which provide a summary of service and include places of birth; the lists are arranged by year of arrival. From the 1820s around 50 per cent of enlisting soldiers were Irish.

Discharge papers 1830–82 and pension records

The discharge records (L/MIL/10/301–2) include soldiers who were wounded, ill, reached the end of service or who managed to buy their way out of the army. Unfortunately, if your ancestor remained in India he is less likely to appear here. For those who returned to Britain or a British colony there are descriptions, including place of origin and service details.

There are pension records for some soldiers in L/AG/23/2, arranged by Presidency.

EIC soldiers' discharge papers 1859–61 are indexed in L/MIL/10/303–317 (Bengal), L/MIL/11, 277–281 (Madras) and L/MIL/12/281–286 (Bombay). The indexes are on the open-access shelves.

From 1861 the European regiments (as opposed to the Native regiments) of the Presidency Armies were incorporated into the British Army. Thus if you are looking for someone who served with the Madras Infantry, for example, who was pensioned for long service or injury after 1861, you need to check the British Army Service Records (TNA ref. WO97) which have been digitized on www.findmypast.co.uk. Not all records survive but several do; even for those who were pensioned in India and chose to remain in residence there.

Pension records

Pension records for the East India Company's armies (1814–75) are held at TNA in series WO23. Registers of EIC and Indian Army pensions (1849–76) can be found in WO23/17–23. Army pensioners in India (1772–1899) are in WO120/135, 69 and 70 but can be found in Crowder, *British Army Pensioners Abroad, 1712–1899* and on the FIBIS online database. See WO25/3137 for registers of pensions paid to former EIC soldiers who served from 1824 to 1856.

Civil and Military Pension Funds began in the eighteenth century, with some continuing until the 1890s. Membership of one of these was compulsory for all EIC servants whose appointments came within the rules of the Fund. Details vary but some of these records can be useful to genealogists in listing details of EIC officers and soldiers, widows, children and home addresses.

The oldest pension fund was the Lord Clive Military Fund, with pensioners admitted from 1770 to *c*1885. This fund provided benefits for all ranks and their widows but not their children: the registers are in L/AG/23/2, with the payment books mainly in series L/AG/21/10. These were 'ex gratia' pensions, awarded on a charitable basis, often to widows in the UK. An index of officers, chaplains and surgeons whose widows received pensions in the UK from this fund is at IOR LISTS 204.

Additionally, there were Presidency funds whose records may provide details of subscribers' marriages, wives, children, birth and death dates. They were open to officers, surgeons and chaplains and the details are:

- the Bengal Military Fund existed up to 1862 (index L/AG/23/ 6/12 to L/AG/23/6/12)
- the Bengal Military orphan society up to 1862 (index L/AG/23/ 6/12 to names of subscribers' children in L/AG/23/6/12)
- the Madras Military Pension Fund up to 1862 (volume of edited information from L/AG/23/10 is in AAS at IOR.355.332)
- the Madras Medical Fund for widows of surgeons and veterinary surgeons up to 1870 (L/AG/23/9).

For further information on the recipients of these funds, see Chapter 7.

Indian Army (IA) 1858–1947

The Indian Army became the official military power in India after the reorganization that followed the Mutiny. It incorporated the EIC Armies and was kept separate from the British Army until 1903.

The Indian Army kept the three Presidency divisions and comprised Indian non-commissioned officers and other ranks commanded by British officers. Unattached officers served a year with a British regiment, learning Indian languages and the way of life in India before being allowed to join an Indian Army regiment.

Indian Army records can generally be found in L/MIL/14.

OFFICERS

From 1859 to 1861, the Addiscombe Seminary was known as the Royal India Military College. In 1861 it closed and Indian Army cadets were subsequently trained at the Sandhurst and Woolwich military academies. Records of service for Sandhurst cadets commissioned onto the Army Unattached List 1901–40 are held in series L/MIL/9/303–19 in the India Office Records (index Z/L/MIL/9/3 for 1902–14) and can be consulted up to 1947. There is an index to the application forms in AAS (IOR LISTS 209b), also online via A2A.

Major-General Reid. (personal collection of Valmay Young)

Indian Army officer in India with his family c1900. (Paul Reed)

There are open-access indexes to names in officers' service records 1860–93 in L/MIL/10/75–102 for the Bengal Army, L/MIL/11/73–92 for the Madras Army and L/MIL/12/88–101 for the Bombay Army. Some officers from 1858–1930 received Queen's India Cadetships. Their application forms are held in L/MIL/9/292–302. Names in these and in the records of the King's India Cadetships (nominations 1908–39) are indexed in L/MIL/7/13090–13205 and on open-access shelves in Asian and African Studies.

For officers, sergeants and conductors serving in the Indian Army from 1900–47, you will find indexes to their records of service in L/MIL/14. Annual Unattached Lists for the Presidency Armies 1859–1907 (L/MIL/ 10, 11 & 12) include ages and places of birth but those for the Indian Army from 1908–44 (L/MIL/14) only give information on recruitment and current posting. For Queen's India Cadetships 1858–1930, application forms giving details of each candidate are held in L/MIL/ 9/292–302.

Further information on officers and the station of regiments is held in the *Indian Army List*, of which the British Library holds copies for 1901, 1902, 1905–39.

The Indian Military Service Family Pension Fund, which ran from 1873–1914, was open to officers, surgeons and chaplains of the Indian Army. It paid benefits to widows and children. Details of families 1873–93 are in L/AG/23/16/4–9 (index L/AG/23/16/10) and later family registers are in L/AG/23/16/37–41 (index L/AG/23/16/42–42).

British Army

Alongside the Company Armies were European Regiments. Following the reorganization of British India after the Mutiny, major changes were made to the armies. In 1859 the European Regiments became Regiments of the Line, and the Company's Artillery and Engineers became part of the Royal Artillery and Royal Engineers. Together these units comprised the British Army in India.

Many British regiments served in India throughout the *Raj*, with officers either staying in India or returning there almost immediately when one battalion left home to be replaced by another of the same regiment. Their military records are held at TNA.

British Library Records of the British Army in India can generally be found in L/MIL/15, although most are held at TNA.

Soldier of the RAMC in India c1900, name unknown. (Paul Reed)

OFFICERS

For officers, checks can be made in the British *Army List*, copies of which can be found at TNA, the British Library (in IOR/L/MIL/17/1), the National Army Museum and other major libraries.

Promotions and other notices concerning British Army officers appear in the *London Gazette*.

The British Library holds information on officers of regiments in India 1806–65, officers formerly on the Indian Establishment who transferred to the British Army 1863–8 (or from British to Indian 1859–61), and some embarkation and disembarkation lists of 1871–89 and 1909–14.

There is a card index at TNA relating to records held in series WO25/3215–3219 and WO76 which includes the names of officers. Those holding a commission in the Indian Army on 1 November 1871 can be found in the papers of the Army Purchase Commission, and the registers of East India Company pensions are held in series WO23/17–23.

Details of officer cadets who trained at the Royal Military Academy Woolwich (1790–93; 1799–1805; 1820–1939) and the Royal Military College Sandhurst (1800–1964) can be located via the online database http://archive.sandhurstcollection.org.uk.

OTHER RANKS

Embarkation Lists for ordinary soldiers 1860–1914 can be found in L/MIL/15/38–48.

For ordinary soldiers, the Bombay Register of European Soldiers in the HC Service 1795–1839 (A–K) in series L/MIL/12/109 is very useful, particularly as it includes place of origin.

Service records of soldiers and NCOs discharged to pension before 1913 are found in the WO97 series which has been indexed on www.findmypast.co.uk. However, if your relative died in service or his papers were somehow lost or destroyed, you will have to rely on muster and pay lists to trace his service back.

Muster lists are also held at TNA in series WO16. There are musters of regiments in India from 1883–89 in WO16/2772–2786; discharge on return home was recorded in the depot musters of the regiment (WO67), in the musters of the Victoria Hospital, Netley 1863–78 (WO12/13077–13105), or in the musters of the Discharge Depot, Gosport 1875–89 (WO16/2284 and 2888–2905).

You can also use the Monthly Returns to the Adjutant General to discover your ancestor's regiment, if you know where they were based. From here the regimental roll can then be consulted.

The indexes to GRO Military births, marriages and deaths have been digitized on www.findmypast.co.uk and www.familyrelatives.com. For Scotland, Foreign Returns (the Register of Deaths in Foreign Countries 1860–1965), High Commission Returns (from 1964), Service Returns (from 1881) and War Returns are found on www.scotlandspeople.gov.uk.

William Halliday of the Royal Regiment. Marriage and baptism records from the ecclesiastical returns can be used to discover more about the career of an ordinary soldier. As there is no surviving service record for the following William Halliday on findmypast (WO97) or in TNA catalogue (includes WO121 pension discharge documents), it would appear that he either died in service or that a pension record has not survived. However, from his marriage entry (N/2/10 f. 353) we learn that William was an Acting Corporal in HM 2nd Battalion Royal Regiment (Royal Scots, or 1st Regiment of Foot) and a bachelor based in Bangalore when he married a widow, Martha Taylor, in Bangalore on 8 November 1826. From his daughter Eliza's baptism record of 1 August 1827 (N/2/ 10 f.158), we learn that between November 1826 and August 1827, William Halliday had been promoted to Corporal. By 4 November 1829 when his son Alexander was baptized in Bangalore (N/2/12 f.127), William had been demoted to a Private in the Royal Regiment. Secondary sources, like regimental histories and Army Lists, can help to fill in details such as the posting of the 2nd Battalion Royal Regiment to Bangalore between July 1826 and July 1830, and its departure from India in 1831. Surviving musters or pay books for the regiment can also be used to fill in gaps in a soldier's service record.

Medals and honours
TNA also hold details of medals, prizes and courts martial. Some of these have been indexed onto family history websites, such as www. ancestry.co.uk and www.findmypast.co.uk. Further information on these may also be found in newspapers such as the *London Gazette*, *The Times* or even local newspapers. As most local newspapers are not indexed a search would require knowledge of a date.

First World War

In the Great War of 1914–18 both Europeans and Indians volunteered for action.

Indian Army Officers of the First World War who were on leave or retired became officers in the short-staffed regular Army or the new Territorial Force regiments. Surviving records are held at TNA in series WO338 (with IA instead of regiment), WO339 and WO374.

There is an open-access index to names in L/MIL/9/435–623 Temporary Commissions and Indian Army Reserve of Officers Entry Papers and Release Dates 1917–21.

The pre-commission records of British Army other ranks who were later commissioned into the Indian Army are at TNA in WO339/139092–139906. The post-commission records are held in the India Office Records at the British Library.

The surviving service records, pension records and medal roll index cards of British Army non-commissioned officers and other ranks who served in the First World War but did not serve in the Second World War have been digitized on www.ancestry.co.uk. The originals are held at TNA but are too delicate to view. The Medal Index cards include those serving in the Indian and British Armies and sometimes provide the address of the next-of-kin, which can be useful if no service (pension) record survives.

Lord Kitchener had been appointed Commander-in-Chief of India in 1903. Among his many reforms was the establishment of an officer training college within India. This was to be the equivalent of the Staff College at Camberley (founded 1802) in the UK but would save the expense of sending those born or living in India to England for training. The new college was founded in 1905 at Deolali but moved to Quetta in 1907, becoming the Staff College, Quetta. From September 1915 until 1919 Quetta served as a Cadet College, training officers for war commission in the British and Indian Armies. Now known as the Command and Staff College, Quetta counts illustrious officers such as Montgomery, Auchinleck and Slim among its alumni. See http://www.dssc.gov.in/history/The%20Quetta%20Heritage.pdf.

Lieutenant O'Donnell, Indian Army officer, WWI. (Paul Reed)

Wellington College was established as a branch of the Quetta College in June 1915 at Wellington in the Nilgiri Hills of Madras to help train greater numbers of cadets for the war and was then closed. After this, according to the Indian Ministry of Defence, 'The Army School of Education was established in the year 1920 with its Indian Wing at Belgaum and the British Wing at Wellington (Nilgiris).'[1] After partition in 1947, a permanent base was established at Wellington *cantonment* for what was Quetta Staff College, now the Indian Defences Services Staff College (DSSC); see http://www.dssc.gov.in.

Application forms for Wellington and Quetta cadets of the Indian Army (1915–18) are held at the British Library in L/MIL/9/320–32 and include details of the cadet, his family background and age. An index can be found within each volume.

In the Great War for the first time since 1791 Anglo-Indians were able to serve as officers. A specific Anglo-Indian battalion was also commissioned. Further details can be found in *The Anglo-Indian Force, 1916* (Allahabad, 1918) in IOR/L/MIL/17/5/4318.

One of the best collections of resources and advice for those researching ancestors who served in this war is The Long, Long Trail website http://www.1914-1918.net.

Everyday Military Life in India 1900–47

In the first decades of the twentieth century, military life for those in the Indian Army revolved around the *cantonment*, where fellow officers and their families were regarded as one big family. As in previous decades, son and nephew followed father, uncle and grandfather into military service. British officers had great privileges and opportunities for sport and hunting. John Morris said, 'The Officer's Mess was the centre of regimental life. Here the unmarried officers spent a great deal of their time and had their meals and in particular, dined together every night.'[2]

Life for NCOs and men (British Other Ranks or 'BORS' as they were commonly known) was far more restricted. They tended to be confined to barracks, which had their own bazaars. Often they were not allowed to visit Indian villages, shops and bazaars. The bungalows where they were housed were vast, sleeping up to fifty men, with only a small area around their bed to call their own. They did have *wallahs* to tend to their needs, however: shaving, serving tea, laundering uniforms, and extra snacks (such as fried eggs and sweets) were all provided by local men for a small charge. This and being addressed reverentially by many Indians

Dagshai MQ (cantonment) *– the original is an old, unused postcard, the only information printed on the back being 'Nestor Gianaclis, Ltd., Calcutta'.* (The Army Children Archive (TACA), www.archhistory.co.uk)

as 'soldier-*sahib*', letters from home, and a fortnight's leave every year made life more bearable. Officers, by contrast, were granted six months in England every two years.

The comedian Spike Milligan was born in Ahmednagar to a British Army corporal, and lived on the Poona *cantonment* until 1927 when he left India. He told of the superiority of the officers and the differences between their lives and those of the men:

> I really thought they were gods and never got very close to them without being properly terrified out of my life. They had very loud voices, very proper, were very well turned out and always on horses, always taller than me, doing things with tremendous panache.[3]

Single women were rare on *cantonments*, and men could only marry if space allowed on the married quarters roll. Only 10 per cent of privates were on this roll, compared with 50 per cent of sergeants, 25 per cent of corporals and all warrant officers. Soldiers would attend Railway Institute dances in order to meet girls, many of whom would be Anglo-Indian.

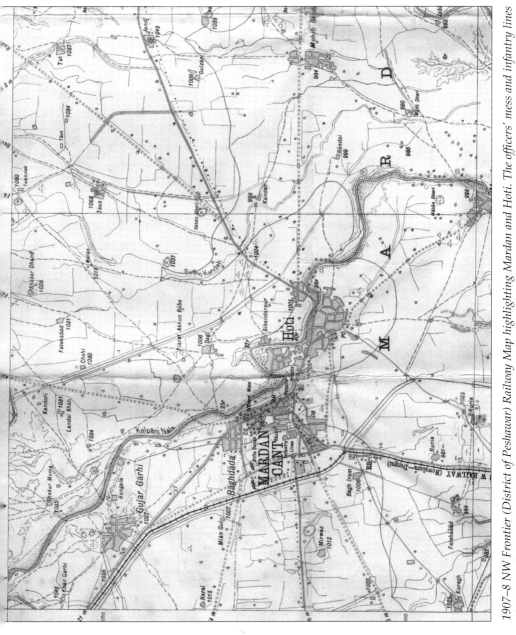

1907–8 NW Frontier (District of Peshawar) Railway Map highlighting Mardan and Hoti. The officers' mess and infantry lines of Mardan Cant are clearly visible. (FIBIS)

Second World War and the Japanese Invasion of Singapore and Burma

The British Empire, which included India, declared war on Germany in September 1939. Europeans and more than 2 million Indians enlisted in the Forces, and millions of men were sent overseas to fight. The Indian Army fought in West Asia, North and East Africa, and Italy; the Royal Indian Air Force fought against the Japanese invasion of Burma.

Careers of Officers in the Royal Indian Air Force and the Royal Air Force in India can be traced through the *Air Force List* Dec 1918–Oct 1948 (L/MIL/17/10/1–300). The *Royal Indian Air Force List* 1941–6 is held in L/MIL/17/10/301–9. Pay accounts of officers can be found in L/AG/20.

For members of the British Royal Air Force (RAF) who served in India 1919–39, there is an index in L/AG/26/12. Payment records of RAF officers 1943–50 are also held in L/AG/20.

Both the British Army in India and the Indian Army were trained to be prepared for war. Serving alongside them in wartime were the Auxiliary Forces India (AFI) – regiments of trained volunteers – and the Army in India Reserve of Officers (AIRO/IARO), which was also active in the First World War. Members of these can be found in the wartime Army Lists, and in the Indian Army service records at the British Library, covering 1900–67 (series L/MIL/14). India was used as an assault and training base throughout this period. However, food and essential materials continued to be exported for use in Britain and for the forces overseas.

Many women volunteered to serve in the war in the Women's Auxiliary Corps (WAC[I]), established by Lady Monkton in 1942, as the Indian equivalent of the Auxiliary Territorial Service. British and Indian women served in the Army, Navy and Air Force in India and Burma. Muriel Wardley (pictured) served as a 2nd subaltern. For confidentiality, women's service records are not available on the open shelves but can be searched for by British Library staff; if your relative is found, career information will be provided. However, officers can be found in the *Indian Army List* April 1943–August 1947.

Recruitment for service in India also took place in Britain. Support in the region became more urgently required after the entry of Japan into the war in December 1941. Nine Indian divisions were posted to the Burma front to try to prevent Japan invading British India. If Japan had captured India, the nation's strategic position could have led to attacks on British posts in the Middle East, and possibly a different outcome to the war.

Muriel Wardley, 1944.
(personal collection of Valmay Young)

As it was, Japan did take Singapore in February 1942, and then invaded the Andaman and Nicobar Islands off the coast of Bengal in March. In April 1942, Japan bombed the Madras ports of Vizagatapam and Cocanada as well as the RAF bases beyond Haflong, and proceeded to advance into Burma. With the fall of Mandalay in May and just one week until the monsoon broke, the Allied forces were compelled to retreat through the jungle into northern India, with some marching 900 miles and accompanied by thousands of exhausted civilians. Around 250,000 refugees escaped but many were stopped by the mid-May monsoon. This left around 40,000 refugees in temporary camps until October, when the weather improved and they were finally able to escape. It is believed that around 13,000 Europeans died between May and October.

In 1942 British geologist Jack Fleming (1900–87) was working in Burma for the Mawchee Mining Company. He had joined the company in the

1920s after studying geology at Birmingham University, and worked as an engineer, plotting and surveying mines. After the invasion, he was held by the Japanese under house arrest. He filled his time translating medieval Latin documents and working on his family history. As a 42-year-old Quaker non-combatant, Fleming was told not to leave the house – the furthest he went was to the veranda. Although Fleming was responsible for the chargers and dynamite in the British copper mines, he kept them hidden from the insurgents and the Japanese. He lived in Burma for five years overall, employing a Karen Christian housekeeper and houseboy. In order to show their power to the Karen people, the Japanese tortured Fleming's houseboy on several occasions by tying him to a tree in the fierce sun. Fleming himself was unharmed but terrorized by what he had seen. Desperate to flee, as soon as he knew the Japanese were defeated he drove as far as he could down the Burma road to Singapore, where he left his car to the houseboy. Fleming resigned from the Mawchee Mining Company in 1946, and lived the remainder of his life peacefully in the Lake District.

By May 1945 Japan had been ousted from most of Burma, a few months before its eventual surrender in August 1945.

However, the toll on Britons in this area had been heavy. Some 60,000 British and Australian prisoners of war had been forced to build a railway along the Thai-Burmese border, and, infamously, along the bridge over the River Kwai. A paper index of Indian Army Prisoners of War 1941–45 is available to consult on the open shelves in AAS. The entries refer to files since destroyed but the images include details of name, rank, regiment, illness, next-of-kin and (if applicable) death.

In TNA series WO345 are 50,000 cards of British servicemen, and WO344 has Liberation questionnaires, completed after the PoWs were freed – the buff papers headed Gp/Gen/J.I/J.2 cover Indian Army officers. However, these records are not comprehensive and not all PoWs completed the questionnaires.

The Imperial War Museum has written, photographic and oral memories of prisoners' experiences in its Discovery History Centre: http://www.iwmcollections.org.uk/qryMain.php. *The Original War Drawings* of *Japanese POW Jack Chalker* and *The War Diaries of 'Weary' Dunlop: Java and the Burma-Thailand Railway, 1942–45* also provide a unique insight into individual PoW experiences. Further details on Far East Prisoner of War (FEPOW) research can be found at http://captivememories.org.uk and private papers in the Cambridge South East Asian Archive.

Deaths of men and women in all the Indian Services and the British Army in both World Wars can be seen in the Commonwealth War

Graves Commission's 'Debt of Honour' database (see www.cwgc.org) and death certificates can be ordered from the GRO (www.gro.gov.uk).

Those who served in Burma received the Burmese Star. For further information on veterans of the Far East campaign, see the Burma Star Association's website: http://www.burmastar.org.uk/index.htm.

If you or your ancestor served in the British Army in the Second World War, or from 1920, you can access service records via the Veterans Agency (http://www.veterans-uk.info/service_records/service_records.html).

INDIAN MEDICAL SERVICE (IMS)

The most comprehensive index of surgeons is D.G. Crawford's *Roll of the Indian Medical Service 1615–1930* (ref OIR.355.435). Details of records of service for surgeons can be found in Baxter's Guide. Surgeons' and Assistant Surgeons' Papers (1804–1914) can be found in reference L/MIL/9/3588, L/MIL/9/358–408, 413–27 and are indexed in AAS (Z/L/MIL/9/5 at IOR LISTS 208d) and online (A2A). Indentures of the appointments of surgeons can be found in the IOR biographical series O/1/1–79 (the Bonds and agreements for EIC officials in the Biographical series 1771–1827).

The Indian Subordinate Medical Service (ISMS or Sub Medical Department) was of a lower status than the IMS. Most employees were recruited locally and were uncovenanted. Thus it is worth checking for a baptism record in the Ecclesiastical Records. Senior members of this service can be found in the respective Army Lists, particularly from 1889–1947, although many can only be located in local directories.

Apothecaries and surgeons in general were employed by government as part of the Military establishment. A Senior Apothecary (later Senior Assistant Surgeon) was a Commissioned Officer with a rank equivalent to either a captain or a lieutenant. Lower-grade Apothecaries (later Assistant Surgeons 1st class), Assistant Apothecaries (later Assistant Surgeons 2nd class) and Sub-Assistant Apothecaries (later Assistant Surgeons 3rd class) were all warrant officers. However, you may find your ancestor described as a 'Civil Apothecary' or surgeon when posted to non-military hospitals or jails.

Useful resources for tracing an Assistant Surgeon's career are the annual Service Histories (1879–1948) in IOR/V/12, using the relevant volume of the locality. Assistant surgeons were also referred to as apothecaries, although this term usually refers to the early twentieth century and before. The Indian Subordinate Medical Department stopped using the term 'Apothecary' in 1894 but later examples can be found.

A relevant local directory can also provide further details on where your ancestor worked, for example, the *Asylum Almanac* for Madras contains lists of hospitals and includes names of staff members such as the IMS Surgeon, Resident Apothecary, Assistant Surgeon, Medical Officer, Hospital Assistant, Steward, Storekeeper, Writer, Matron, Head Nurse and Nurse. Not all staff members are named at each hospital or asylum and the information provided varies through the years but it is worth checking the various indexes in the directories for the duration of your medical ancestor's career.

Further resources on tracing apothecaries and assistant surgeons can be found at http://wiki.fibis.org/index.php?.

Generally, when searching before 1804 for UK appointments of EIC surgeons etc, the following series should be checked:

(i) B series – court minutes
(ii) D series – committee of correspondence (no indexes for 1760s)
(iii) E series – general correspondence
(iv) G series – factory records
(v) P series – proceedings (checked for retirement records)

George William de Rhe-Philipe's *Punjab, N-W.F.P., Kashmir, & Afghanistan Inscriptions on Tombs or Monuments & Biographical Notices of Persons Mentioned* (OIR.929.5) provides useful details on featured surgeons, including career highlights and causes of death.

Veterinary Surgeons' Papers, including petitions, certificates of age and testimonials, survive for 1826–1959 in L/MIL/9/433. Widows and children of surgeons and veterinary surgeons of the Madras Army may be found in the records of the Madras Medical Fund (IOR/L/AG/23/9) up to 1862.

Nurses

Nurses were attached to the Indian Army from 1887. Senior grades are found in the *Indian Army List* after 1891, and Staff Nurses from 1926. Others may be found in local directories. A number of records exist for them among the India Office Records. L/MIL/9/430–432 contains appointments and registers of candidates 1887–1920; L/MIL/7/11617–11803 contains a complementary series of application papers; L/AG/21/13/97 contains pension payment books to retired nurses in the UK 1950–55; and L/AG/20/39/1 contains gratuity payments for nurses released in the UK 1946–47. Records are also available for Voluntary Aid Detachment

(VAD) nurses who served in India during the Second World War but who enlisted in the UK. As these L/MIL/14 personal files are not public, career details can be obtained on request by next-of-kin from the AAS reference section.

The website http://www.scarletfinders.co.uk/18.html contains some information on military nurses who mobilized in India.

A Bengal surgeon: John Davidson of Ravelrig. Like many middle-class Scots of the eighteenth century, Davidson travelled to India to seek his fortune. Thanks to a hardy constitution, some luck, and his perseverance over various inheritances, he managed to achieve this. As a surgeon, his career is well documented. His entry in the *Roll of the Indian Medical Service 1615–1930* reads:

> Davidson, John (a) A.S. 1760. Surg. Chittagong, Mar. 1762.
> Calcutta, 6 May 1766 R. 11 Jan. 1768; (B. Cons.). Living in 1792.
> v. Hist. Of I.M.S. i. 190, 191

This tells us that Davidson was Assistant Surgeon in the Bengal Presidency in 1760; he was promoted to Surgeon in March 1762. From there he was sent to Calcutta on 6 May 1766; he retired on 11 January 1768 and this was mentioned in the Bengal Consultations (Bengal Proceedings: series P); he was still living in 1792 and more details can be found in the *History of the Indian Medical Service.*[4]

In 'Anderson's Narrative of the Massacre at Patna, &c: communi-cated by John Davidson Esq.' (IOR/H/456d 1653–1793) we learn how dangerous life could be for surgeons. The letters explain how William Anderson was 'murdered by order of the *Nabob* Cossim Alli Cawn upon hearing of the defeat of his Army by the Major Adams' on 6 October 1763, the day William Anderson wrote his last letter to Davidson.

IOR/H/192 17561762 (2) pp. 97–8 show Davidson's financially savvy side:

> Mr John Davidson sends in a letter acquainting Us that the late Doctor William Stuart Surgeon at Cossimbazar, who died there about a Month before the Troubles broke out, left A Will wherein he appointed him his Sole Heir and Mr Edward Oakes of that Factory his Executor, who he learns took an Inventory of the Effects of the deceased and sealed it up ... Davidson then alleged that when the Factory at Patna was captured by the Nawab of Bengal in 1763, 'All Mr Stuart's Good's were Plundered and his Papers lost,' thus resulting in the confusion over his estate.

Davidson's persistence ensured he eventually received the benefits of the estate. In 1768, he resigned. Davidson returned to Scotland, where he married Hannah Mackenzie (1751–1818) and sired four children. Their son, Joshua, went on to become President of the Royal College of Physicians in Edinburgh. John Davidson died in 1815, and is buried at Greyfriars Kirkyard, Edinburgh.

Notes
1. http://www.mod.nic.in/rec%26training.
2. Charles Allen, *Plain Tales from the Raj*, pp. 203–4.
3. Ibid., p. 222.
4. D.G. Crawford, *Roll of the Indian Medical Service 1615–1930*, pp. 190–1.

Chapter 6

MERCHANTS AND SHIPS

... in the development of British India, sea power was the basis on which the whole structure was founded.

R.K.H. Brice, Preface to
The History Of The Bengal Pilot Service (1963)

Maritime Ancestors

Britons of all ages, genders and social classes sailed to, from and around the Indian subcontinent and South-East Asia from 1600 to the mid twentieth century for work, adventure, fortune-hunting and social pursuits. Some were sailors or merchants who worked for the East India Company in their own Mercantile Marine, Military Marine or Pilot Services, or, later, under the *Raj* in the Indian Navy. However, not all lived in and worked from India: some were merchant mariners working for British traders and ship-owners; others were in Indian waters in a purely military capacity, serving in the Royal Navy.

The records available for your ancestor will depend on the area in which he or she worked, or on other reasons behind their passage to India.

East India Company Naval Service

The East India Company had its own Mercantile Marine (1600–1834). There were also the Bengal Marine, which included both the Bengal Pilot Service and seafaring commercial and military vessels, and the Bombay Marine, which had a military function although it included a Bombay Pilot Service. The Bombay Marine became the Indian Navy in 1830 but reverted to the Bombay Marine in 1863. In 1877 the Bengal Marine and the Bombay Marine combined to become Her Majesty's Indian Marine, known from 1892 as the Royal Indian Marine. Useful genealogical sources for marine ancestors can be found at http://www.barnettmaritime.co.uk.

The EIC sailed out of London in their own ships – the East Indiamen – from the docks near its headquarters in Leadenhall Street. On board each Indiaman were the commander, as many as six mates, surgeon, purser and midshipmen. There were also inferior officers: boatswain, gunner and carpenter, surgeon's mate, and petty officers. Below them in rank were the caulker, cooper, captain's cook, ship's cook, two stewards, sail-maker, armourer, butcher, baker, poulterer, barber, six quartermasters, mates, servants and fifty seamen. A large ship carried a crew of around 100, whereas the smaller ships were manned by about fifty. The com-manders were allowed some goods for their own personal trade; a privilege they often abused, creating the potential to become very rich. Not all the crew would be British; among the lower ranks there may have been Indian Lascars, Chinese, Germans, Spanish, French and Americans. Many of these left children in India with British or Anglo-Indian women.

The administrative and operational records of all EIC naval services and those that replaced them are found in the L/MAR series in AAS. One of the best places to begin tracing a maritime ancestor who worked for the EIC is in Anthony Farrington's *A Biographical Index of the East India Maritime Service Officers 1600–1834*, which lists the careers of the Honourable East India Company's Maritime Service (HEICMS) officers.

EIC Mercantile Marine
The EIC Mercantile Marine was abolished in 1834. The main source of biographical information on its members is in the Maritime Service Statements that were compiled in 1834 and are now held in L/MAR/ C/894–895. These statements were made to facilitate compensation on the abolition of the marine to officers, surgeons, boatswains, pursers, carpenters and gunners. As well as service records, the statements give details of baptism, marriage, and wives and children.

For Mercantile Marine officers appointed 1780–1820, there are baptism certificates and certificates of age in the indexed volumes of L/MAR/ C/668–70. L/MAR/C/671 contains baptism certificates and certificates of competence for midshipmen appointed 1820–30. L/MAR/C/669–70 contains indexed baptism certificates and certificates of age for marine officers appointed 1780–1820.

Bengal Marine
Records for the Bengal Marine are found in L/MAR/8. L/MAR/8/11 contains a list of Europeans employed in the Bengal Marine Depart-ment, giving name and rank, casualty returns, and condition of pilot

vessels May 1793–December 1833. L/MAR/8/12 contains Statements and abstracts of the Bengal Marine Establishment on 1 May 1834 with lists of European members of staff and their dependants drawing salaries or pensions in 1834. L/MAR/8/13 contains lists of seamen employed by the Bengal Marine Establishment, giving name, vessel to which attached, date and place of discharge and wages due; separate casualty lists give names, vessels to which attached, date and place of casualty and wages due January 1811 to 7 September 1821.

L/MAR/8/14 contains Bengal Marine Department and Steam Engineers Establishment Returns and Casualty Lists September 1848 to December 1852. L/MAR/8/16 contains Staff Lists for the Bengal Marine Establishments, giving name, dates of entry into government service and appointment to present position, monthly and annual rate of pay 21 March 1873 to 31 March 1874. L/MAR/8/18 contains Bengal Civil and Marine Departments Casualty List December 1856 to February 1864. L/MAR/C/762–763 contains Bengal Marine records of service for 1857–59, covering those mariners who fought for the Bengal Naval Brigades during the Indian Mutiny.

Bengal Pilot Service 1669–1948

The Bengal Pilot Service was created in 1669 to guide ships up and down inland waters on the Hooghly River between the Bay of Bengal to the city of Calcutta.

M.H. Beattie's memoir of serving in the Bengal Pilot Service, *On the Hooghly* is on the open shelves of Asian and African Studies. The appendices of his book include lists of branch pilots 1847–57, pilots who joined from 1858–93, and pilots who have joined since 1893. The 1847–88 lists have been digitized on FIBIS: http://search.FIBIS.org/frontis/bin/aps_browse_sources.php?mode=browse_components&id=189&s_id=39. The book itself is in the University of Delhi's digital library at http://library.du.ac.in/xmlui/bitstream/handle/1/2490/Ch01-On%20the%20hooghly%28ch.1-10%29.pdf?sequence=5. Beattie joined the Bengal Pilot Service in 1876 at 14 years old on a training ship and retired in 1913. According to Beattie, the Government of India was recruiting for the Service from the training ships in this period but, 'Under the Honourable East India Company the appointments lay with the Directors, who gave them to the sons of their friends. Later, boys were chosen from the Bluecoat School and from Greenwich.'[1]

Beattie describes the characters and appearance of several branch pilots with whom he either worked or had heard about. There were four grades of branch pilot: Branch, Senior Master, Junior Master and Mate. Each pilot had an Indian servant.

The India Office Records contain Lists of Pilots in the Bengal Pilot Service 1796–1836 in L/MAR/8/6, nominations in L/MAR/8/4, Entry Papers for the Bengal Pilot Service 31 March 1818 to 5 August 1844 in L/MAR/8/1, and Lists of Rank of Volunteers appointed to the Bengal Pilot Service 1838–61 in L/MAR/8/5. There are further records of Bengal Pilots including seniority lists in the L/MAR/8 series. Some may be found in the V/12 series.

The most comprehensive history is the unpublished text by Capt. G.T. Labey and Capt. R.K.H Brice, *The Bengal Pilot Service* held at NMM in THS/12/1–9. This explores all areas of the service and is useful for those researching its employees: Appendix G, for example, includes obituaries of those who worked in the Pilot services.

NMM also houses the Percy-Smith Collection (MS 88/006) on the EIC's mariners, which must be ordered in advance of a visit. The collection is separate from the Percy-Smith Collection at SOG and includes 'Particulars of certificates granted by the Government of Calcutta up to December 1902 to Masters, Mates and Engineers in Mercantile Marine'. These records are most useful to those researching river pilots who were born in India and served in the late nineteenth or early twentieth centuries. The entries include the pilot's name, date and place of birth, class of certificate, certificate number and its date of granting. These records divide into: Colonial Certificates of competency; Local (Foreign Trade) Certificates of competency; Local (Home Trade) Certificates of competency; Local Certificates of Service; Local (Inland) Certificates of Service; Local (Inland) Certificates of Competency. There are also index cards (Item 29) for the Bengal Medical (1740–1914, surnames A–H only); Bengal Orphans (1780–1840); Bengal Marine and Bengal Pilots (1700–1914). The Museum's collections can be searched at http://www.nmm.ac.uk/collections/explore/listCollections.cfm. Further information on Bengal Pilots can be found in the journal, *Bengal Past and Present*.

Joseph Richardson, Bengal Branch Pilot. Joseph Richardson volunteered for the service on 12 January 1807, when he was around 12 years old. I found a letter written by Joseph Richardson in L/MAR/8/1 Entry Papers for the Bengal Pilot Service 31 March 1818 to 5 August 1844. This record was extremely fragile and contained letters and baptism certificates. The letter itself referred to Joseph's son, Daniel but also highlighted Joseph's poor health. In L/MAR/8/6 Lists of Pilots in the Bengal Pilot Service 1796–1836 I discovered the following entry for Joseph Richardson:

Name	Volunteers	2nd Mates	1st Mates	Masters	Branch Pilot	Remarks
Richardson, Joseph	12 Jany 1807	21 March 1812	8 Dec 1814	1 Sept. 1820	Branch	–

As can be seen, he passed his 2nd Mates' certificate on 21 March 1812. An announcement in the *Asiatic Journal & Monthly Miscellany, Vol. 32* confirmed that he died in Ceylon: *Registers – Calcutta: Deaths: 1840, April 2, At Colombo, Mr Joseph Richardson, Branch Pilot, aged 45.*

Bombay Marine 1613–1830

As the Bombay Marine operated in a military capacity, you should find information relevant to your ancestor's work in published histories of the EIC's military activities in this period. Other useful resources on this are the books *The Bombay Country Ships* and *Free Mariners and the Country Ships* (OIR.382.094 Open Access).

Biographical information may be found via the Bombay Marine cards from Hodson's index, which are held at NMM.

For more information on the Bombay Marine and the Indian Navy, see the FIBIwiki guide at http://wiki.FIBIS.org/index.php?title=Ships_of_the_Bombay_Marine_and_Indian_Navy.

Indian Navy (1830–63) and the Royal Indian Marine/Navy (1877–1948)

The Indian Navy was created in 1830 but disbanded in 1863. It was replaced by a new non-military Bombay Marine. The Bengal Marine and the Bombay Marine joined together as HM Indian Marine in 1877, and this eventually became the Royal Indian Marine in 1892. In 1935 it was renamed as the Royal Indian Navy and continued thus until 1948.

For Indian Navy officers and warrant officers who were serving between 1860 and 1945, there are service statements in series L/MIL/9/1–9 (the index is on the open-access shelves in Asian and African Studies IOR LISTS 212).

Further Sources

In 1654 the Company built Poplar (later the East India) Chapel as a chapel of ease in which its sailors and staff could pray before setting sail; some too would come to be buried. The Chapel later became used by family members of those in Company service, as well as local business-men and those connected to the shipbuilding industry. Its parish records were transferred to All Saints, Poplar, and are now held at the London Metropolitan Archives; for alternative records of those buried there, see Tony Fuller's *Memorial Inscriptions at the East India Company Chapel, Poplar*.

The Poplar Pension Fund was open to officers and seamen of the EIC Mercantile Marine and their families. The application papers for 1809–38 are held in IOR/L/MAR/C/789–840 (index in L/MAR/C/785–86). They include complete service records, marriage details, and baptisms of children. The Poplar Pensioners worshipped at St Matthias, and lived in nearby almshouses.

British Merchant Seamen

There is no one set of merchant seamen records and searching for a specific name in the records that do exist can be difficult. Further details on this subject can be found in *My Ancestor was a Merchant Seaman* (SOG, 2004) and *Records of Merchant Shipping and Seamen* by K. Smith, C.T. and M.J. Watts.

Before 1835 there are no service records as such but many merchant seamen can be found in the Trinity House Papers 1787–1854. These papers include petitions, giving the names of merchant seamen or their families who requested aid from Trinity House (an organization responsible for lighthouses and charitable funds for seamen); Apprenticeship Indentures and Miscellaneous papers. The originals are held at SOG but the Calendars to the papers have been uploaded to www.findmypast.co.uk.

From 1747–1853 you can check the ships' musters for merchant ships, which list crewmen and voyages. These are held at TNA in series BT 98 but are unindexed and sometimes do not give the crewmen's names. For 1835–44 there are Crew Lists in BT 98. They are filed by the ship's Port of Registry; although unindexed, they do give the name, age, place of birth, quality, and brief career history of each seaman.

From 1845–54 there is an Alphabetical Register of Masters in BT 115. There are similar Crew Lists in BT 98 for 1854–56, and also records for 1857–60. For this period the records are arranged by the ship's Official Number (ON), which can be found in the *Mercantile Navy List* or *Lloyds Register*. An index to the news section of *Lloyds List* can be searched by name of seaman or ship via the Guildhall's website at http://www.cityoflondon.gov.uk/lloydslist. This can reveal details such as crew members being lost at sea or ships wrecked.

From 1852 there are some surviving log books, which list the men's names, conduct, illnesses, deaths, desertion and punishment. Births on board are also given. The records are in BT 99, except for 1902–19 where they are held in BT 165.

From 1861–1938 and 1951–92, Crew Lists are scattered; mostly at NMM, while the remainder are in BT 99 (searchable on the Catalogue), BT 100 and BT 165. Second World War Crew Lists can be found in BT 381, BT 380 and BT 387. For further details and a searchable index created by the Maritime History Archive at the University of Newfoundland see www.crewlist.org.uk, also http://www.mun.ca/mha.

From 1845 useful records of officers' service are held at TNA in references BT 115 (Alphabetical Register of Masters), BT 143 (indexed Certificates of Competency & Service, Miscellaneous) and BT 6/218–219 (Certificates). These Masters and Mates are also listed in *Lloyd's Register of Shipping* and may be found in the *London*, *Edinburgh* and *Belfast Gazettes* (www.gazettes-online.co.uk). Registers of Certificates can be found in references BT 122 (Certificates of Competency, Masters and Mates, Foreign Trade 1845–1900), BT 123 (Certificates of Competency, Masters and Mates of Steamships, Foreign Trade 1881–1921), BT 124 (Certificates of Competency, Masters and Mates, Foreign Trade 1850–1925), BT 125 (Certificates of Competency, Masters and Mates, Home Trade 1854–88), and BT 126 (Certificates of Competency, Masters and Mates, Colonial 1870–1921). An index to these is available in BT 127.

At TNA, Certificates of Engineers are available from 1862: BT 139 (Registers of Certificates of Competency, Engineers 1861–1921), BT 140 (Registers of Certificates of Competency, Engineers, Colonial 1870–1921), and BT 141 (Registers of Certificates of Service, Engineers 1862–1921). The BT 141 Indexes to Registers of Certificates of Competency and Service, Engineers 1862–1921 cover those named in BT 139, 140 and 142. Further certificates are held at NMM.

Lloyd's Captain Register (1851–1947) is now held at London Metropolitan Archives. It has been indexed from 1869 (retrospective for masters and mates still sailing in 1869) to 1911, and can be found online at http://www.history.ac.uk/gh/capintro.htm.

Sea Service records from 1913 include registers and renewals of certificates of competency of master and mates in BT 317; and masters, mates and engineers in BT 318. Merchant Navy Seamen index cards CR1, CR2 and CR10 (1928–1941) can be searched on Find My Past. Some include a photograph of the seaman in question.

Registration of Merchant Seamen became compulsory with the Merchant Shipping Act 1835. Registers of Service 1835–57 can be found at TNA in

BT 120, BT 112, with an index in BT 119. Further registers are in BT 113 (index BT 114) and BT 116.

Details of some medals and honours can be found in the *London Gazette* (http://www.london-gazette.co.uk) or TNA's Catalogue can be searched by name in T335 for Second World War Merchant Navy Gallantry awards. The Royal Marine Medal Roll 1914–20 has been digitized on www.findmypast.co.uk.

NMM holds staff records for three companies of P&O: the Peninsular and Oriental Steam Navigation Co. Ltd., British India Steam Navigation Co. Ltd. and the Orient Steam Navigation Co. Ltd.

Samuel (Sam) Jenkinson Fitzakerley (1874–1961). Originally from Sunderland, Sam Fitzakerley was a Chief Engineer for Brocklebanks, a shipping company that had traded with India since 1813. From the period of the First World War until his retirement in 1937, Sam sailed the route between Liverpool and India. The company suffered heavy losses in both world wars. As Sam knew many of the men who were lost during the Second World War, he listened with great sadness as their names were read out on the wireless. Fortunately several lives were also saved, even where ships were lost. In 1941 the SS *Mahseer* was torpedoed by a magnetic mine in the Thames Estuary while returning from India with essential metals for the war effort. All ninety-seven crew members survived. More on Brocklebank's ships can be found at http://www.theshipslist.com/ships/lines/brock.html.

Royal Navy

Royal Naval Officers' service records 1756–1917 and warrant officers' service records 1830–1931 are held in ADM 196 at TNA, and have been digitized at http://www.nationalarchives.gov.uk/documentsonline/adm196.asp. Certificates of service for warrant officers and ratings who served 1802–94 and applied for pension are held in ADM 129, and have been indexed by name on the Catalogue. Ratings' pension records can be found in ADM 73 and ADM 29 and are similarly indexed. Details on ratings for those who entered the service 1853–1923 can be found in the Registers of Seamen's Services in ADM 139 and ADM 188 or online at http://www.nationalarchives.gov.uk/documentsonline/royal-navy-service.asp.

If a service record cannot be found, the career of your naval ancestor could be traced through surviving ships' muster and pay books in ADM 31–39, ADM 115, ADM 117 and ADM 119. If you know the name of a ship on which he served, you can search the Catalogue for this using the above references.

- Commissioned Sea Officers of the Royal Navy 1660–1815 can be searched on www.ancestry.co.uk. The Royal Navy medal rolls for campaign, long service and good conduct have also been digitized here from ADM 171. Officers' careers can be traced through the (bi)annual *Navy Lists*.
- Casualties of the Royal Navy 1914–19 and those of the First World War Royal Naval Division can be found at www.findmypast. co.uk.
- Royal Naval Reserve Officers' service records 1862–1920 are held in ADM 240. Ratings' service records for the Royal Naval Reserve 1909–55 are currently held by the Fleet Air Arm Museum (http:// www.fleetairarm.com) but indexes to these and the service records 1860–1909 are held at TNA in BT 377.
- Veterans Agency (http://www.veterans-uk.info/service_records/ service_records.html) holds details of how next-of-kin can obtain the service records of any Royal Naval officer who served from May 1917 from the Ministry of Defence.

Records of Ships

One of the most comprehensive guides to EIC ships is Charles Hardy's *Register of Ships 1760–1933* and includes names of all surgeons employed, the captain and senior officers, and the ports sailed for each ship in each sailing season. There are also lists of East India Commanders. The book can be read online at www.archive.org.

Further information on the ships sailed in by your ancestors can be found in Anthony J. Farrington's ships' index, *Catalogue of East India Company Ships' Journals and Logs 1600–1834* in L/MAR/A–B in AAS. For example, we can learn more about the experiences of Ensign Jarrard Strickland (see Chapter 5) as the index tells us that the *Northampton* on which he sailed to India was owned by Moses Agar and that she sailed from Portsmouth on 9 September 1801 under Captain Robert Barker arriving at Bombay on 11 February 1802. From reports in *The Naval Chronicle Vol VI* July–December 1801 and Charles Hardy's *A register of ships, employed in the service of the Honorable the United East India Company From the year 1780 to 1810*, we discover that the *Northampton* had been built at Mestaer's yard at Rotherhithe in 1800, and that her owner Moses Agar leased her to the East India Company on 25 March 1801 for a basic fee of £20,165 for one return voyage to India. We also learn her size: she had just three decks, and measured 123 feet 6 inches in length with a beam of 32 feet 1 inch, and weighed 542 tons.

Further details of other EIC ships, including names of ship owners and captains, can be found online at www.eicships.info or in FIBIS Fact File No. 7 by Richard Morgan.

Most of the ships sailed by the EIC were not owned by the Company but were instead chartered by them from wealthy shareholders for a set number of journeys. These ship-owners were known collectively as the Shipping Interest. All manner of ships were sailed by the British in India, including teak-built ships, steamers, ancient crocks, opium clippers, tea clippers, cruisers and steamers.

The East Indiamen were enormous, awe-inspiring vessels, usually built on the Thames. To protect from potential danger they were armed with at least twelve guns. There were *regular* Indiamen, which sailed for twelve or fourteen years – at least six voyages – and *extra* ships that were leased for one voyage at a time. These were the smallest ships (around 500 tons) and carried goods such as rice, sugar and saltpetre. The 800- and 1,200-ton ships carried the more valuable piece goods and silks. There were around 100 Indiamen in the Company's fleet.

Many of the teak ships were built in India (especially Surat, Bombay and Burma) from native wood. Ship-building, with British involvement, became an important industry.

Navigational instruments improved in the seventeenth century and the increasing number of charts for the seas helped sailors to reach their destinations successfully. By the late nineteenth century, ships were able to estimate their date of arrival within a day or two.

More ships sailed from economically important Calcutta and Bombay than from Madras, which had a more strategic value.

Merchants and Trade

Historical changes from pirates to financiers and employers
Although early sailors in the EIC had been pirates, the Company's ships were soon to be at the mercy of international pirates during the long, dangerous journey to and from India.

Until 1813 the Company held a complete monopoly on trade with the East, to the benefit of Britain. Goods from Bengal, in particular, flooded out of India while Britain sent little in return. Britain received cloth and other cotton products, silks, sugar, rice, wood, indigo, tobacco, alcohol, betel, saltpetre, salt, minerals and coffee. In return India received men, woollen items and iron. Despite heavy taxation in Bengal, there was little money left for further goods as the coffers had been emptied by the many wars. More information can be found in Cyril Northcote Parkinson's *The Trade Winds: A study of British overseas trade during the French Wars 1793–1815*.

Travel to India

At this time ships sailed around the Cape, powered only by the monsoon trade winds. The round trip to India was 12,000 miles. After the EIC's trade monopoly with India ended in 1813, other companies took advantage of the opportunity of this trade. Merchant mariners from various private companies sailed to and from India from this period until after partition.

Country Trade and Free Mariners

The East India Company did not just trade with India. The trade between various oriental ports – known as the Country Trade – enabled even greater profits. The triangular nature of trade was formed by the British exporting manufactures (wool, tin) to China, shipping opium, tea, silk and porcelain from China to India, and then Indian raw materials and Chinese goods to Britain. Notably, the Free Mariners did not trade with Europe or anywhere west of the Cape – instead, the goods reached Britain via EIC ships and employees.

This trade was not monopolized and from the seventeenth century many privately-owned British merchant ships based in India traded with other Eastern countries under licence from the EIC. These Country Ships were the best designed and built ships on the seas, owned and manned by Free Mariner officers. The EIC's influence on the trade led to many licences being granted to former employees.

The Country Trade became less significant after China banned the importation of opium in 1800. Although those involved in this trade endured many risks, there were great rewards for the owners and officers to be made in a short period of time. As the Company was reluctant to give up the lucrative opium trade, it devised a scheme whereby the Country Ships smuggled opium into China, while official EIC ships did not carry the drug. All this ended in 1833 with the loss of the Company's monopoly rights over the Chinese trade.

Further information can be found on Free Mariners and other maritime and merchant ancestors in Bullock's *Directory of Non Official Europeans in India (1780–1820) – lists of Europeans and Anglo-Indians not in the King's Service*. A copy is held at SOG. Few records remain, although you may find some ancestors mentioned in directories, the Home Miscellaneous

Series in the British Library (IOR/H), and the Marine Department records (IOR/L/MAR/C/67478). For an account of the life of one officer, see *Free Mariner: John Adolphus Pope in the East Indies 1786–1821.*

The Tea Trade

In the eighteenth century, the most profitable trade with the East was that with China in tea. The drink had become very fashionable in Britain, and was championed by writers such as Samuel Johnson and Oliver Goldsmith. Dr Johnson's friend and biographer, James Boswell wrote of the doctor's relationship with the beverage: 'With tea he cheered himself in the morning; with tea he solaced himself in the evening.'[2] Happily for the EIC, many others shared his enthusiasm.

Assam history
From 1685 the EIC traded in tea from Canton; the plant, it was believed, grew only in China. However, in the 1820s two EIC employees, the explorer and opium trader, Major Robert Bruce and his brother Charles, discovered tea growing in Tezore district, Assam. Shortly afterwards, it was found in the mountains near Munipore by David Scott. These discoveries were timely, as relations between China and Britain in this period were tense, threatening the supply of tea. After specimens had been examined in India by botanist Dr N. Wallich and confirmed to be *Camellia Sinensis*, the government began experimental cultivation of the tea-plant in the northern and hill provinces of India. By 1833, when the EIC lost its trade monopoly with China under the Charter Act, the prospect of a tea trade with India began to take shape. In January 1834 Governor Bentinck wrote of the advantage of such a trade and appointed a Tea Committee to investigate. There followed a 'tea rush' in 1840s Britain. Allegedly, in 1839 tea grown in India was sold for the first time at London auctions in Mincing Lane; in fact, the Empire Tea Centenary was celebrated in January 1939 in the City of London. According to the *Merchants' magazine and commercial review*, however, the first public sale in Britain of Assam tea (Souchong and Pekoe) took place in London in 1840.

Tea companies
By 1839 the EIC's tea plantations were being run by the Assam Tea Company. The companies were based at tea gardens, and more details on them, their owners, managers, assistants and agents can be found in contemporary directories. By 1859 there were tea estates not just in Assam

and (from 1855) Cachar but also in Travacore, Kangra Valley, Darjeeling, Terai, the Dooars, Chittagong and in the Nilgiri Hills. All of these were run by Europeans, supported by Indian staff.

Records of tea-planter ancestors can be found in the records of the respective tea estates. One of the most useful sets of these for family historians is that of the letter-books of the firm James Finlay & Co. held in the Scottish Business Archives at the University of Glasgow. The index to staff members can be seen at http://www.gla.ac.uk/media/media_169147_en.pdf.

Dedicated directories of planters can also help locate ancestors not found in more general directories. Among those stored at the British Library are *The planting directory of India and Ceylon*, 1879 (IOL: T10348), *Planting directory of Southern India*, 1896, 1924–25, 1928, 1937, 1940, 1965 (IOL: ST1447), *D'Vauz's Burma pocket almanac and directory*, 1886–87, 1889, 1891 (IOL: ST1403), *Hyderabad almanac and directory*, 1874–76 (IOL: ST1449), *Lahore directory*, 1923 (IOL: ST1448), *Hayes' Mysore and Coorg directory*, 1884–85, 1904 (IOL: ST1402), *Tenasserim and Martaban almanac and directory*, 1857 (IOL: ST1430) and *The Travancore directory*, 1910, 1932, 1938, 1949(1), lists of European and American residents (IOL: ST1429).

On the FIBIS database there is a searchable index of more than 200 names taken from the diaries of Samuel Cleland Davidson, tea-planters in Cachar 1865–75: http://search.FIBIS.org/frontis/bin/aps_browse_sources.php?mode=browse_dataset&id=628&s_id=806.

George Barker, *A Tea Planter's Life in Assam* gives an insight into everyday life on a tea estate in the nineteenth century and can be read online at www.archive.org.

The memories of Jim Robinson's life on a tea estate by the Sessa River near Dibrugargh in the 1960s (which can be read at www.koi-hai.com) include:

All around us were the tea gardens with their neat lines of shade trees painted white up their trunks to prevent white spider harming the crop of 'two leaves and a bud' that the pluckers methodically collected from May to November. We had wildlife all around us. A tiger regularly used the gate at the end of the drive as a scratching post. South of the bungalow, a leopard patrolled the *nullas* or drains around the tea bushes. Pythons and cobras bathed on the lawn in the sun. Above all there was the magic of the river… During the rainy season you could barely see more than a few yards. The sandy banks fell like mini avalanches into the swollen water, uprooting trees and carrying away animals.

George Collett with tiger cubs. (personal collection of Valmay Young)

For more details on tea-traders in India see the FIBIS guide: http://wiki.FIBIS.org/index.php?title=Tea_Plantation.

Coffee

Coffee plantations were established in Malabar in southern India from the seventeenth century, although coffee had been traded in India (and taken to Britain) from the sixteenth century via the Country Trade with the Mochs in Yemen.

Alfred Cruse was born in Wiltshire in 1843 but sailed to India in 1860 as an employee of Alpin Grant Fowler, the proprietor of coffee estates in the Neilgherry Hills. He was still working as a coffee-planter at the time of his marriage in Madras in 1864 but shortly afterwards he took the

98

position of Inspector of Works with the Madras Railway. Alfred never returned to coffee-planting: he died of cholera on 7 October 1884, and his obituary appears in *Minutes of the Proceedings of the Institution of Civil Engineers* (Vol. I, xxxii; Session 1884–85. Part iv).

Travel To and From India

Passenger lists

There were no specific passenger ships to India before the second half of the nineteenth century. Before this passengers travelled on either merchant or military vessels. Passenger lists are variable in their survival and usefulness. Of those that do survive, some can be detailed – with full names, addresses and years of birth – whereas others simply give initials and the port of disembarkation. In India this tended to be the port of Calcutta, Bombay or Madras. Most ships for India embarked from London or Southampton. Once the rail link was established, some London-based passengers travelled by rail to board at Southampton.

The earliest surviving passenger lists outside of the military embarkation lists (see Chapter 5) are held at the British Library. Before 1833 passengers to India had to seek permission from the EIC's directors. Copies of these permits can be found in the Court Minutes (B series) and Despatches in series E (in the East India Company Letter-books, 1625– 1753 in E/3/84–111). Indexes are available in AAS. For passengers to St Helena, check the St Helena Public Consultations: G/32.

Otherwise, there are no official passenger records before the late nineteenth century. However, lists of passages can be found in early directories, and some give the names of passengers arrived. They are unindexed but some have been digitized on the FIBIS database.

Later passenger lists are held at TNA. Some 24 million indexed Outward Passenger lists from Britain 1890–1960 from their BT27 series have been digitized at http://www.ancestorsonboard.com. The British incoming ship passenger records 1878–1960 (from TNA's BT 26 series) can be found on www.ancestry.co.uk. Find My Past or www.findmypast. co.uk has indexes of some overseas births, marriages and deaths as well as the outgoing passenger lists of Ancestors On Board.

Some female ancestors may have travelled to India as part of the so-called 'fishing fleet' – unmarried young women who travelled to India for the autumn/winter social season, in the hope of 'catching' an eligible husband (ideally from the upper echelons of the Indian Civil Service or Armed Forces). It is worth searching the indexes for these women and the somewhat cruelly named 'returned empties' (those who failed to find a husband).

Alternative lists

Many of the ships' logs in the Asian and African Collections contain passenger lists. These show that it was not just EIC employees who travelled on the ships.

The logs of East Indiamen 1702–1834 in L/MAR/B include outgoing and incoming passengers. Passengers to and from India 1838–45 can be found in L/MAR/C/887, and a register of deposits on account of native servants accompanying passengers to England 1838–58.

There are several passenger lists at TNA. Jeremy Wraith's list of Army Officers embarking for India (and elsewhere) taken from WO25/3503 series has been digitized on the FIBIS database.

Dangers of sea travel

Travel to and from India was fraught with danger, with many ancestors having been last recorded before a sea passage. However, by investigating further into the likely passage taken, it may be possible to discover what happened to your ancestor.

Shipwreck was a common problem. It is possible to identify ships which were wrecked through the ship records mentioned above, as well as through newspaper databases such as that of *The Times* which regularly recorded the movement of ships.

Many ancestors were taken ill on board the ships with illnesses varying from sea-sickness to outbreaks of cholera or plague, often arising from the length of the journey and the cramped conditions on board. Until the Suez Canal opened in 1869 the passage to India around the Cape of Good Hope lasted for four months, although it could take up to six in poor weather. From the 1830s it was possible to travel by ship to Alexandria in Egypt, then by rail to Port Suez, completing the journey by ship: steamships only were used for the sea journeys on this route. Unlike other vessels travelling to India in this period, steamships could carry more than 100 passengers. Experiences of early voyages from primary sources are found at the FIBIS database http://wiki.FIBIS.org/index.php?title=HEIC_Early_Voyages.

Later the journey could take just three weeks, and the level of first-class travel dramatically increased. The more exclusive passengers who knew to reserve the cooler north-facing cabins going to and from India became known as POSH: they travelled Port Out Starboard Home.

Map of Mail Routes. (courtesy of Dr Geoffrey Eibl-Kaye)

The various wars and diplomatic conflicts that occurred throughout Britain's time in India led to many dangers and deaths. Not only were ships attacked and sunk throughout the centuries by enemies of Britain but some passengers fell victim to capture by military enemies, disgruntled Indian leaders (in the seventeenth and eighteenth centuries), or mercenary pirates. Over the years Britons at sea were attacked, killed and taken prisoner by the French, the Dutch, the Portuguese, Indian princes, the Japanese and pirates of varying nationalities.

For those who managed to survive all of the aforementioned dangers but remained at sea, there was the possibly even more terrifying prospect of being attacked by predatory sea or river creatures, such as sharks or the crocodiles of the Hooghly.

In the years when Britain was at war with France the risk of attack by French ships whether in European waters or off the Île de France was high; Lieutenant Jarrard Strickland was taken prisoner by the French on his return to Britain in 1808.

Records of births/marriages/deaths at sea

General Register Office of England and Wales indexes to Marine Registers of Births and Deaths 1837–1965 are indexed at www.familyrelatives. com. www.findmypast.co.uk holds numerous records for events at sea, including Births at Sea 1854–87, Marriages at Sea 1854–87 and Deaths at Sea 1854–90. Also www.thegenealogist.co.uk hosts GRO Miscellaneous Foreign Returns (1831–1964), which include some events on ships.

The Scottish Marine Register from 1855 records deaths of merchant sailors usually resident in Scotland, as well as deaths of Royal Navy and Royal Marine personnel during wartime (including members of the Royal Naval Reserve, the Royal Naval Volunteer Reserve and the RNLI). This can be searched at www.scotlandspeople.gov.uk.

For earlier periods, it is worth searching the announcements in directories. It is also sensible to check newspaper databases or newspapers for the relevant area if you have a limited time period for the event. For more details on military deaths at sea, look through the relevant muster rolls and pay books for the entry of your ancestor.

Notes
1. M.H. Beattie, *On the Hooghly.*
2. James Boswell, *The life of Samuel Johnson, LL.D., including a Journal of his tour to the Hebrides,* vol. 9, p. 170.

Chapter 7

RELIGION, CEMETERIES AND SCHOOLS

... of all the memories I hold those of my childhood in India the most dear.

George Roche, *Childhood in India:
Tales from Sholapur* (1994)

Ecclesiastical Records

The Ecclesiastical Records comprise the returns of baptisms, marriages and burials, relating mainly to European and Anglo-Indian Christians in India, Burma and other areas administrated by the East India Company and the Government of India. These are the most commonly used records by family historians and they cover an estimated 70 per cent of the Christian baptism, marriage and burial registers in India. Those original records were copied and returned to London for administrative purposes.

The records are indexed at the British Library in Z/N series: Returns of Baptisms, Marriages and Burials 1698–1969. The index of surnames is arranged by first letter only, and then by year of event up to 1909 but is fully alphabetical from 1910. There is no index for women in the marriage registers up to 1897. Sadly, these records do not include copies of all the church registers in India. Nonconformist church records and Roman Catholic records are included but some Catholic records are listed separately. The returns are incomplete as not all churches made and returned copies, and of the copies that were made, some were lost or destroyed.

The returns were transmitted to the India Office by chaplains and Government of India ministers, primarily for record purposes. There are separate indexes for the three Indian Presidencies (Bengal 1713–1948; Madras 1698–1948; Bombay 1709–1948). There are also separate indexes

ARCHDIOCESE OF CALCUTTA

CERTIFICATE OF BAPTISM

DATE OF BAPTISM		1st January 1946
DATE OF BIRTH		26th December 1945
SEX		Boy
CHILD'S CHRISTIAN NAME		Noel Robert.
PARENTS' NAMES	CHRISTIAN	Robert Lionel. - Emily.
	SURNAME	GUNTHER
ABODE		Khargpur
FATHER'S RANK OR PROFESSION		B.N.R.Workshops.
SPONSORS		Roy Enright, Khargpur. Mary Enright, Khargpur.
WHERE BAPTISED		Khargpur, Rly. Hospital .
CLERGYMAN OFFICIATING		Rev. P.H. Sharpe

Certified that the above is a true extract from the Register of Baptisms kept at the Church of the Sacred Heart, Khargpur, Eastern Rly., W. Bengal.

The 7th of January 19 55.

Confirmed on 3.8.52, Kidderpore.

Married on xxxxxx

Vicar.

Baptism certificate. (Noel Gunther)

for Burma (1937–57); India and Pakistan (1949–68). The records cover events in St Helena (1767–1835), Fort Marlborough (1759–1825), Penang (1799–1829), Macao and Whampoa (1820–33), Kuwait (1937–61), and Aden (1840–1969). All the surviving registers have been microfilmed and can be consulted in AAS. FIBIS volunteer Sylvia Murphy has compiled an index for Bombay marriages, which is held in a black folder in the reading room. This index includes brides as well as grooms. Many of these records have been indexed on www.familysearch.org and micro-films can be accessed at Family search centres; also the complete set of Ecclesiastical Records will be digitized on www.findmypast.co.uk by early 2012.

Records that were created in India but whose copies were not returned or did not reach London may still be held with the church. It is worth contacting the Archdiocese of the church you are researching to see if they can locate the records for you. Do note, however, that many records were not sent back from the railway hill stations.

Non-Anglican Records and Places of Worship

The early ecclesiastical returns are all Anglican as the EIC only employed men of that faith. Finding records of Catholics or nonconformists up to the late eighteenth century can thus be difficult. Later records are also sparse: the Church of India, Burma and Ceylon (previously the Anglican Church in India) separated from the Church of England in 1930 but remained an Anglican church. After this change, fewer records were returned to London and thus fewer baptisms, marriages and deaths can be found in the India Office Records for British Indians after 1930. Names of churches, chapels and other places of worship can be identified through directories.

Roman Catholic records can be found in larger numbers from the 1830s as a consequence of the 1829 Catholic Emancipation in England and Wales. Many Anglo-Indians of Portuguese, Italian and French descent were Catholics, as were the many Irish soldiers who supported the British and Indian Armies of the period. Although the records were created separately, they are indexed with Anglican events in the Ecclesiastical Records. Before Emancipation, many Irish Catholic soldiers used the nonconformist missionary chapels. Unfortunately, several non-conformist churches refused to send copies of records to London. Most Church of Scotland records were returned; only those of St Andrew's Church of Scotland in Calcutta were not: http://standrewschurch-kolkata.org/index.html.

SOG holds several church records from India, some of which do not feature in the Ecclesiastical Records. Areas covered include Amritsar, Benares, Bengal Presidency Registers, Calcutta, Canwar, Cochin, Coorg, Dalhousie, Delhi, Fatehgarh Camp, Gulmarg, Gurdaspur, Jhansi, Jutogh, Kalka, Kasauli, Madras, Meerut, Ootacamund, Quilon, Sanawar, Simla, Srinagar, Sudasheoghur, Tranquebar, Trivandrum and Bencoolen (Sumatra). It also holds an RC Directory for the Archdiocese of Agra, Allahabad & Lahore 1908 which includes school prospectuses and the names of priests, nuns and missionaries.

For more detail on this topic including links to addresses of bishops and archdioceses, see the FIBIS website: http://wiki.fibis.org/index. php?title=Church_records.

Religions in India

India had been home to numerous religions for centuries before the British arrived. Even after the advent of the EIC, Indian religions continued unaffected well into the eighteenth century.

The three ancient religions were Hinduism, Buddhism and Jainism. As these had originated in India they were valued deeply by their adherents. These differed from Christianity with Hindus and Jains worshipping a variety of gods and goddesses. Buddhism is focused on living a balanced life according to four Noble Truths, although, like Hindus, Buddhists believe in *karma*. *Karma* comes from the Sanskrit for 'action'. It is described in Buddhist teaching as follows:

> for every event that occurs, there will follow another event whose existence was caused by the first, and this second event will be pleasant or unpleasant according as its cause was skilful (good) or unskilful (bad). 'Unskilful' in this context refers to an act committed by a person driven by greed, resistance or delusion.

Jainism was founded in the sixth century BC by Mahavira as a reaction against the way Hinduism was being organized in that period and the Brahmin (warrior) rule. It is a non-violent religion, to the extent that its adherents practise strict vegetarianism.

Later, in the eighth century, Arab traders brought Islam to India; by the Middle Ages, it grew further with the invasion of Muslims. Following the Mughal invasion in the sixteenth century, Islam became the second most-followed faith, after Hinduism (and its various forms). Unlike Hinduism, Islam is a monotheistic religion, with Muslims worshipping *Allah*, the God Almighty.

Zoroastrians arrived in the tenth century from Iran, and their faith is based upon a philosophy of man's responsibility to choose between the opposing forces of good and evil. Most adherents became known by the more commonly used name of Parsees, and settled in Bombay.

Sikhism was founded in the sixteenth century in Punjab, northern India, and involves the worship of one God. Sikhs do not support the caste system but do share with Hindus the ideas of *karma* and rebirth.

Other lesser-known religions were created over the centuries. There was also a presence in India of Christianity (particularly Roman Catholicism around Kerala and Madras) and Judaism before the arrival of the EIC. For further details on religion in India see V.S. Naipaul, *India*.

Conversion To and From Christianity

During the Governorship of Warren Hastings, the male-dominated British Indian society began to take an interest in not only Indian women but also their languages and faiths. Although many British officers and merchants had children with local women and several married, there were few who converted officially to Indian religions. The few that did included James Achilles Kirkpatrick who converted to Islam (see p. 29), and Major-General Charles Stuart (*c*1758–1828) of the EIC, who converted to Hinduism.

'Hindoo Stuart', as he became known, was an enthusiastic student of Indian languages and customs; he admired Hinduism above all for its morality and he converted to vegetarianism. He was also popular with Indian people as demonstrated in the following death announcement from *The Naval and Military Magazine*, volume 4, 1828:

> ... he was beloved on account of his generosity and kindness to all who applied for his aid, and his constant charity to the poor, of whom a hundred destitute objects were for years back daily fed at his expense. Through life he was distinguished by a peculiar benignity of manners and cheerfulness of disposition, qualities which never forsook him, and which, combined with his varied information, and honourable character, acquired for him the esteem of those who had the pleasure of his acquaintance; although they might smile sometimes at a perceptible tinge of eccentricity.[1]

The East India Company was against interfering in the cultural lives of the Indian population, except in using their religious difference to pit different rulers against each other. The Company was concerned chiefly with profit, and as forced conversion was bad for diplomacy and thus business, missionary activity was banned in India. Even in the 1820s, the Governor of Madras, Thomas Munro, was against converting the Indian population. He wrote in a letter of 19 July 1824: 'When I read, as I sometimes do, of a measure by which a large province has been

St Andrew's Church, Madras. (http://en.wikipedia.org/wiki/File:St_Andrews_Church_The_Kirk.jpg)

suddenly improved, or a race of semi-barbarians civilized almost to Quakerism, I throw away the book.'

Records in the UK and in the English language of those who converted from Christianity are most likely to be found in obituaries in conemporary magazines. Many of the sources used by William Dalrymple in his exploration of the conversion of James Kirkpatrick are discussed in detail in *White Mughals*. Other prominent converts to Islam include the Resident at Delhi, Sir David Ochterlony (*Nasir-ud-Daula*), and William Linnaeus Gardner, whose sons included a Christian clergyman who doubled as an Urdu and Persian poet.

Records of those who converted to Christianity are held with other Christian records, and many are found in the Ecclesiastical Records.

Missionaries and Religious Leaders

In the 1800s evangelism was growing. After the former EIC director Charles Grant was converted, it seemed that it would not be long until India would be open to missionaries. Despite the fears of other more financially-motivated directors and governors like Munro, Evangelicals across Britain voiced fears of the superstitions they believed Indian religions encouraged. This missionary zeal was not popular within India, especially outside of Calcutta. Orientalist Charles Stuart was critical of European Evangelicals in his *Vindication of the Hindoos* (1808), describing them as 'obnoxious', and their mission as 'impolitic, inexpedient, dangerous, unwise and insane'. However, when the EIC lost its control of missionary activity in 1813 (along with its charter), religious groups seized the opportunity to convert India to Christianity. Also in 1813 a bishop and three archdeacons were appointed to India for the first time.

Lower-level officials promoted evangelical Christianity and Utilitarian rationality but many senior officers did nothing to encourage them. Too many of these senior Britons feared the pious interference in the indulgent and decadent lives they were able to live while they were away from home. Other, usually middle-class Britons, however, were keen to promote not just Christianity but also Western ways into the Indian population. Religion plus education was the key, argued proponents such as the historian (and son of the slavery abolitionist and Evangelical Zachary Macaulay) Thomas Macaulay. This was a view shared by the Governor-General William Bentinck; his power ensured that an era of Anglican cultural colonialism now began in British India.

One aspect of this cultural colonialism that has been viewed favourably by modern eyes was the abolition of both *suttee* (or *sati*) and female infanticide. It was Bentinck who banned *suttee* – the Hindu practice of a widowed woman immolating herself on her husband's funeral pyre – across the Bengal Presidency in 1829. In Bengal alone there were 7,941 deaths by *suttee* between 1813 and 1825.[2]

By 1832, India was home to fifty-eight Church Missionary Society preachers.

A useful place to begin a search for missionary ancestors is in a local directory for the area in which they were based. The Ecclesiastical Establishment section of directories lists nonconformist churches with contact names, such as 'American Free-will Baptists 4. Phillips, J ... Jelasore; Baptists. 20. Phillips, T ... Muttra' in the 1852 Scott & Co.'s *Bengal Directory & Register*. Bengal directories list missionaries from 1835 and clergy of all denominations from 1837. Madras directories list Protestant missionaries from 1833 and Catholic clergy from 1838, Bombay directories list missionaries from 1839 and Catholic clergy from 1852. *Thacker's* lists clergy of all denominations 1885–1942. For brief biographies of missionaries up to 1886, see *The Indian Missionary Directory: Memorial Volume*.

The Mundus online gateway to missionary collections at http://www.mundus.ac.uk can be searched by person and also by place. Thus, even if your ancestor is not listed by name, you can browse through a list of 108 records on missionaries in India that may provide further information on your ancestor's activities. Also Adam Matthew digital database (http://www.amdigital.co.uk) has many digitized records from East and South Asia, including some concerning missionaries.

One of the most comprehensive collections of missionary records can be found at SOAS Library in London. These include the Archives of the Conference of British Missionary Societies (1872–1973), records of the Commonwealth Missionary Society (formerly Congregational or Colonial) 1836–1966, the Methodist Missionary Society Library, and the London Missionary Society.

Brief biographies of chaplains can be found in S. MacNally's *Chaplains of the EIC*, and for Anglican clergyman from 1858 see www.crockford.org.uk which features biographies of more than 20,000 clergy. Many religious leaders were educated at universities and some alumni records can be found with the respective institution or at www.ancestry.co.uk.

There are several useful missionary magazines that contain biographical details of missionaries and those who supported their mission. The Branch Pilot Joseph Richardson, mentioned in Chapter 6, was a supporter of the Old Church District Charitable Society in Calcutta. The *Calcutta Christian Observer* of 1840 (pp. 409–13), which has been digitized on Google Books, contains a detailed memoriam to Joseph, stating not just his occupation and where he died but details of his character, 'one of its most efficient and invaluable members' and of the illness that caused his death:

> He suffered most intensely during the last three months of his life. The severe spasms which he endured became of daily occurrence, and sometimes lasted for a long time, and even for two or three days with more or less pain … latterly his feet and legs swelled so, that he could not move, but he remained cheerful till the last. The day before his death he sat up in bed, endeavouring to write to one of his children which letter was left unfinished, for on the morning of the 9th instant, death came suddenly upon him.

Also, of his funeral:

> He was buried in Colombo, several Civilians, Merchants and Officers following his remains; which were carried to the grave by a party of H.M. 95th Regt.: the union flag was used as a pall, and his friends did all in their power to shew their respect for him by thus honoring the burial.[3]

Cemeteries

As not all burial records survive in Britain, you may find useful details on tombstone (monumental) inscriptions, some of which have been indexed in published works. Many of these works covering 1848–1946 are held on the open shelves at the British Library in the Monumental Inscriptions and Monuments series V/27/74. For British burials in India see http://indian-cemeteries.org. A partial index to monumental inscriptions is available to search at the British Association for Cemeteries in South Asia (BACSA)'s website: www.bacsa.org.uk. Many monument inscriptions, some including photographs, can be found on the FIBIS database http://search.fibis.org/frontis/bin/aps_browse_sources.php?mode=browse_classes&source_class=148.

Your ancestor's name, grave, or cemetery may be found on the Access to Archives website http://www.nationalarchives.gov.uk/A2A. Many of the records indexed on this site can be examined in person at the

111

British Library, although some need to be ordered in advance (see below). Many other names may be found in books of inscriptions uploaded to Google Books or the Internet Archive.

For example, a search on 'monumental inscriptions' reveals a number of indexes, including 'Indian Monumental Inscriptions Nos 1578 to 2000 and Index' *c*1781–1935. Bound reprints from Bengal Past and Present with typed index prepared in 1938 in British Library Collections, Private Papers; MSS Eur F146/9.

Some cemeteries, such as that at Meerut, are well maintained and may be visited.

Memorial to Daniel Francis Gunther (1819–1900). (Noel Gunther)

More resources for researching your ancestors' graves, both at home and in India, can be found in FIBIS Fact File No. 6: *Graves in British India* by Richard Morgan.

Schools and Orphans

Many children of British-born or British middle- and upper-class parents were sent to Britain for their schooling. As with Rudyard Kipling (see Chapter 4), one reason for this was to avoid them being 'country-bred' and thus excluded from senior positions in British Indian employment and society in adult life. Another was to avoid the heat, monsoons and consequent illnesses that often killed British children. Military children of other ranks were often given a rudimentary education at regimental schools. When researching middle- and upper-class children, however, it is important to check British sources for the school records of your ancestors.

The records of many schools can be found via Access to Archives (http://www.nationalarchives.gov.uk/A2A). Several public or private schools hold excellent records; alumni of schools like Charterhouse, Westminster, St Paul's and some grammar schools may also be found at www.thegenealogist.co.uk or in the School Lists and Yearbook section on www.ancestry.co.uk.

Surviving records of state schools, such as admission/discharge registers and log books, may also be found in local records offices. The names of schools in a specific area and period can be found in local directories, or at http://www.british-history.ac.uk/Default.aspx. You may also find your scholar ancestor on the UK census, either resident in the school or staying with family or others outside term-time.

For those who remained in India, a similar process of research can be made. Directories list British schools in India as well as providing details of convents and orphanages where many European children were educated. However, records are harder to find for those who attended schools rather than orphan asylums. Some records have been uploaded onto the FIBIS database and can be searched by name of pupil: http://search.fibis.org/frontis/bin/aps_browse_sources.php?mode= browse_classes&source_class=229. These records include various school registers and names of Calcutta Free School prizes in 1878. More information can be found in *A Brief History of the Calcutta Free School up to 1920* in *Collation of Pamphlets on Anglo-Indians* (1921, Free School Society).

For more recent alumni, check if there are surviving alumni associations. For example, alumni of St Thomas's School, Kidderpore, Kolkata,

George and Winnie Wheeler. (personal collection of Valmay Young)

West Bengal, India, have the St Thomas Old Pupils Association to help them keep in touch.

Orphan Asylums

The high mortality rate among British Indians inevitably created a great number of orphans. For seventeenth-century orphans see E/3/40 No. 4689, which gives a list of orphans at Bombay for 31 December 1679. Malayan records of the Malaccan Orphan Chamber (*c*1685–1835) are found in R/9.

Many orphans were cared for through the various pension funds mentioned in Chapter 5. Several other orphans were sent to Britain to be cared for by relatives and may be found in parish records or later censuses. For those that remained there are number of useful records.

Pension funds
Lord Clive's Pension Fund

> was established by the EIC in 1770 using prize monies Lord Clive
> received from the battle of Plassey ... the money would be put in
> trust in EIC bonds with the idea that it would produce an annual
> interest of 8 per cent and that amount would be sufficient to cover
> the cost of pensions to European soldiers who had been in the
> Company's troops.[4]

William Kirkpatrick, half-brother of James Kirkpatrick (see p. 29)
founded the Military Orphan Society in 1782. The Society was created
in keeping with the Company's aims and contemporary practices of the
upper classes back in Britain. Aside from the caring aspect there was also
a political element in that many of the children in the eighteenth-century
asylums were Anglo-Indian. Several children were deliberately taken
from their Indian mothers after their fathers had died in order to give
them a British upbringing at one of the orphan schools. This could
explain why some of the children here were not complete orphans; some
had lost their mothers only and a very small percentage had both living
parents.

Girls at the asylums usually stayed in India, either in service or
married from their asylums (often to soldiers). The sons of officers tended
to enlist in their father's regiment, while the sons of other ranks may have
entered the armies as drummers or fifers, entered the EIC as Writers, or
been apprenticed.

Bengal asylums
Orphans in Bengal can often be found described on marriage or other
records as 'Ward of LOS' or sometimes just 'LOS' after their name. This
stands for Lower Orphan School, which stood in Calcutta.

Ghosh writes of how the Lower and Upper Orphan Schools came to be
named:

> ... in 1783, with the Court's approval, the managers of the orphan
> society were granted Rs. 3 per month and Rs. 40,000 to build an
> orphanage for 300 children. Pay stoppages were authorized from
> each soldier under the company's command. 1785 Howrah, the
> children of officers occupied the upper floors of the building ...
> while the children of the lower ranks moved into the ground floor
> and the terms Upper and Lower School came into parlance. By
> then, there were 96 students in the Upper School and 160 in the

Lower school. In 1790, the school moved yet again; this time the Upper School moved across the river to Kidderpore house, located in Alipore, which was south of Calcutta in the district known as 24 Parganahs (image in *Twelve Views of Calcutta* by W. Baillie 1794; plate nos 5 and 11 are of upper and lower school).[5]

This marked the separation of the schools: by 1790, there were 300 pupils in the Lower School, and by 1803 there were more than 500. In 1815 the school moved to Alipore. Few records of the Upper School survive as it was maintained as a private institution, paid for from the pension funds; children here were the offspring of officers, medical staff and ranks above sergeant. However, the LOS was part funded by the Company, and more details on these orphan asylums can be found in the Military Department Proceedings at the National Archives of India (NAI).

Some details can be found in the records of the Bengal Military Orphan Society lists of orphans (IOR/L/AG/23/7/7) but they do not include names of orphans before 1823. Names of some orphans from these records 1820–57 can be found on the FIBIS database; details include their dates of birth, dates of admission, discharges, and names of fathers. There are also names of orphans here from 1798.

Up to 1815 many children from LOS were buried at the Orphan Burial Ground, Howrah (in the grounds of the school). Children from the UOS were buried in the Orphan Burial Ground, Kidderpore House. Later burials for LOS children may be found at Fort William or the Alipore Military Burying Ground.

There is some correspondence beginning in 1815 regarding the Bengal Orphans in IOR/F/4/504/12102. Several documents pertaining to the schools have been digitized on Google Books.

Other useful sources are *The History, Design and Present State of the Religious, Benevolent and Charitable Institutions Founded by The British In Calcutta* by Charles Lushington and *Poor Relations: The Making of a Eurasian Community in British India 1773–1833* by Christopher J. Hawes.

Deposits for orphans of named officers can be found in some editions of the *Asiatic Journal and Monthly Register* which has been digitized on Google Books. One good example of this is taken from a longer list in Vol. X, July–December 1820 (p. 587):

Children of the late Capt. Walter Mayberry
Samuel W. Skardon, orphan son of the late Lieut. Fire-Worker
    S. Skardon, being balance of his share
G. Thompson, son of the late Conductor R. Thompson
Anne Mawbey, daughter of the late Capt. Mawbey

Children of the late Lieut. W. Hiuksman
V. Clydesdale, daughter of the late Assist. Surg. J.Clydesdale
C. Cumming, daughter of the late Capt. R. Cumming
A.E. Cresswell, daughter of the late Lieut. W. Cresswell
H. Hearsey, daughter of the late Lieut. Col. Hearsey
W. Pickett, son of the late Lieut. W. Pickett
Children of the late Capt. W.H. Royle …

Also in Bengal were two of the four co-educational asylum schools founded by (or in the name of) Sir Henry Montgomery Lawrence (1806–57), a former army officer and Resident at Lahore; the Lawrence Military Asylum was opened at Sanawar in 1846. The site was near Kussowli (Kasauli) in the Himalayas and not far from the *Raj* retreat of Simla. For those whose ancestors were school-age orphans between 1848–58, the *Brief Account of Past Ten Years of the Institution Established in the Himalayas by Sir H.M. Lawrence for the Orphan and Other Children of European Soldiers Serving, Or Having Served in India*, H.M. Lawrence Military Asylum (1858) which has been digitized on Google Books should prove useful. The website for the current school is http://sanawar.edu.in.

The other Bengal Lawrence Military Asylum was opened in Ghora Ghali, near the Murree Hills in 1860. This school still exists and its website is http://www.lawrence.edu.pk.

Bombay
The Central Schools in Bombay funded by the Bombay Education Society provided education for children of the poor. The schools moved to the suburb of Bycullah in the 1820s, and made provision for orphans at the Military Asylum. Only one of the Lawrence Asylums was in Bombay; it was founded at the hill station of Mount Abu in Rajasthan in 1856.

Madras
The Madras Military Female Asylum was situated in Poonamallee. However, there are records of boys at this site also. The FIBIS database holds names of orphans at this school for 1839. The Madras Military Male Asylum was situated in Mount Road, Madras; names from 1835 are on the FIBIS site. There are further records from the Military Asylum for 1825–26. From 1858 the Lawrence Military Asylum opened at Lovedale near Ootacamund. The following year this Asylum combined with the Military Male Orphan Asylum. As with all Asylums, not all of the pupils here were orphans; several were here as their fathers were posted away

with their regiments. For more information, see *Lovedale: The Lawrence Memorial Royal Military School, South India: a personal account* by Max Cocker. The school still exists and its website is http://webarcindia.com/lawrence.

More detail on life at the orphan asylum schools can be found in a series of articles by Maureen Evers in the FIBIS journals of 2009–10 and at the FIBIwiki page http://wiki.fibis.org/index.php?title=Orphans.

Asylum Press

In Madras the Asylum Press was run by the boys at the Madras Military Asylum, who printed government publications including directories and ephemera. The *Asylum Press Almanac* ran from 1863–1936 and can be found in the British Library at OIR.954.8.

At nearby shelf-mark OIR.354.5 is another directory; this from the Bengal Asylum: *List of East India Company's Civil and Military Servants.*

Notes

1. Death announcement in *The Naval and military magazine*, vol. 4, 1828.
2. Sakuntala Narasimhan, *Sati: widow-burning in India*, quoted by Matthew White, 'Selected Death Tolls for Wars, Massacres and Atrocities Before the 20th Century', p. 2 (July 2005), Historical Atlas of the 20th Century (self-published, 1998–2005).
3. *The Calcutta Christian Observer* of 1840, pp. 409–13.
4. Durba Ghosh, *Sex and the Family in Colonial India: The Making of Empire*, p. 217.
5. Ibid., pp. 228–9.

Lucknow Girl Guides Proficiency Badges, Emily Upshon.

Chapter 8

RAILWAYS

... the complete permeation of these climes of the sun by a magnificent system of railway communication would present a series of public monuments vastly surpassing in real grandeur the aqueducts of Rome, the pyramids of Egypt, the Great Wall of China, the temples, palaces and mausoleums of the great Moghul monuments.

Lord Dalhousie, 1853

The railway system is one of the greatest legacies of British rule in India and a masterpiece of civil engineering. With its 40,000 miles of track, 7,000 stations and staff of more than 1.5 million, the railway industry remains one of India's largest employers. The first official railway passenger journey in Britain took place on the Stockton to Darlington Railway in 1825. In British India, the first passenger train journey was to Thane in 1853. After this, railways were built all over the country.

It is believed that the railway acted as the unifying force of India. Railway work in its various forms became a popular form of employment under the *Raj* for Europeans in India, and many travelled from Britain for well-paid positions. Not all personnel records survive for all railway companies but it is possible to explore your railway ancestor's career through a number of useful sources.

History of the Railways in India

In 1847 35-year-old James Broun-Ramsay, 1st Marquis of Dalhousie, was appointed Governor-General of India. His utilitarian philosophy and desire to modernize India over his eight-year rule have been much criticized; at the time, his policies of expansion and the Doctrine of Lapse[1] caused great resentment and are believed to have led to the Mutiny. However, there is no doubting Dalhousie's administrative capabilities and his greatest legacy may well be the improved communications he established in seeking to unify India. Besides an extended road network and improvements to mail and telegraph services, Dalhousie regarded the British invention of the railway as being the ideal medium to achieve this unification.

As President of the Board of Trade in Britain between 1845 and 1846, Lord Dalhousie had promoted the progress of the railways there. Britain in the 1840s had seen a period known as Railway Mania, where many made fortunes by investing in the railways although others had suffered great losses. On his arrival in India in 1848 Dalhousie found not one piece of railway track had been laid, despite surveys having been done and two railway companies having been created in the 1840s. The East Indian Railway Company (EIR) which ran from Calcutta was formed privately in 1845, re-constituted in 1847 and incorporated by Act of Parliament in 1849. The Great Indian Peninsula Railway (GIPR) was formed at a similar time, running from Bombay. Both companies were British and registered in London.

Dalhousie's great dream was to link the railways of these two companies so that a single line spread across the country linking Bombay to Calcutta. He ensured that the military engineers of the EIC's armies used their skills to begin the grand project in earnest, and that wealthy bankers, traders and shipping companies invested in creating the railways with guarantees of a 5 per cent return. The investors would also gain from improved trade for their businesses and access to Indian coal for powering the new steamships: by 1860, there were twenty-eight steam engines running on the coal belt alone. Britons were eager to invest and, by 1875, they had contributed around £95 million.

The first railway ran from Calcutta and was designed by EIR engineer George Turnbull. The first train ran to Roorkee carrying building materials and, on 16 April 1853, the GIPR railway opened by carrying the first official passengers 21 miles from Bombay to Thane. In August 1854, Howrah station opened to transport passengers to Hooghly. Calcutta in particular was to benefit enormously from the railway's contribution to export trade. Without the EIR, eastern India would have been unlikely to see the economic development that later occurred. The inexpensive rates of third-class travel also opened India up to millions of the population.

One of the most important British engineers in the expansion of the railways was Robert Maitland Brereton, who eventually became Chief Engineer of the GIPR. On 7 March 1870 his work finally achieved Dalhousie's aim of linking the EIR to the GIPR when the GIPR line reached that of the EIR at Jubbulpore. Brereton oversaw the creation of a vast network of 4,000 miles that enabled direct travel between the major cities of Calcutta and Bombay. Brereton's Bombay to Calcutta railway

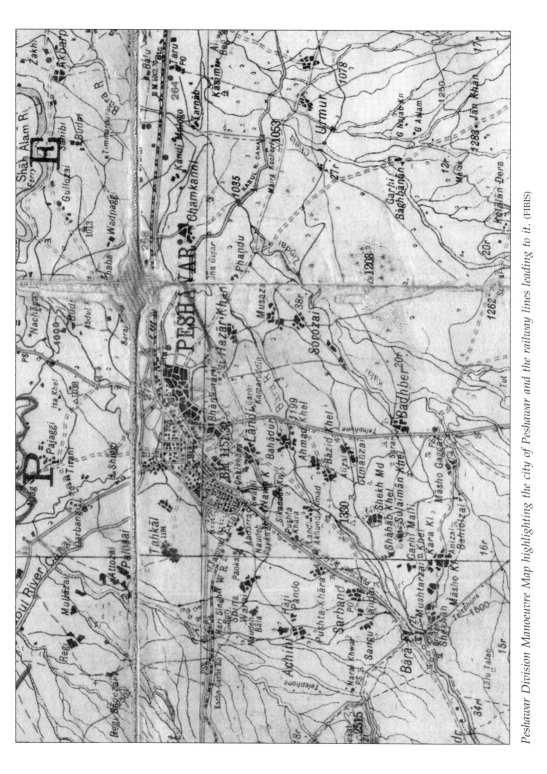

Peshawar Division Manoeuvre Map highlighting the city of Peshawar and the railway lines leading to it. (FIBIS)

line was the base from which further railway lines could be built, spreading in all directions across the country. You can read about Brereton's memories of building the railway at archive.org: http://www.archive.org/stream/reminiscencesofo00brer.

Once each railway was completed its ownership could pass to the government but management tended to remain with the private company that had created it. Gradually, most railways became owned by the British Indian Government but many were leased back to private companies to manage. The GIPR came under state control in 1900, and in 1901 a Railway Board was established. After this the Indian railway began to make a profit. The railways also became more sophisticated with the emergence of electric trains.

By 1921 the Indian railway system was the fourth largest in the world but had been run down during the First World War. Between 1907 and 1925 the government owned and managed almost all railways; the remainder were owned by Princely States or private companies. Also from this period more Indians were employed, and locomotives began to be built in India itself. This was a boom period for the railways but was swiftly followed by the difficult years of the economic depression of the 1930s. During the Second World War railway workshops were used for munitions. The government interceded further by nationalizing the major systems in 1945, and by 1946 owned all the railways of India.

Life as a railway worker

Railway ancestors include engineers, surveyors, builders, supervisors, managers, clerks, inspectors, stokers, drivers, boilermakers, blacksmiths, fitters, carriage and wagon men, station-masters, guards, ticket-inspectors and many more. They included men of varying social class, educational background and origin. Their lives varied too, between occupation and era. The everyday life of a builder in the 1850s, for example, was very different from an engineer in the 1870s or a blacksmith in the 1900s. Different roles became more or less important as the railway system grew.

While the first railways were being built, experienced builders were sent over from Britain to supervise local labourers. Later, engineers, drivers, fitters and so on were enticed to India by good wages and conditions; wages in India were often higher than for the equivalent role back in Britain. However, traffic staff tended to be employed within India; as many of these had served in the army it may be worth checking records of soldiers and NCOs for your traffic ancestor's name (see

Chapter 5). Other railway ancestors may be found in military records as volunteers with the railway units of the armed forces.

There was a great sense of camaraderie among railway workers, even between Indians of different regions or religions. For Anglo-Indians in particular the railway (and its associated trades) was a major employer; it was they, alongside labourers from Britain, who had laid the first sleepers in the 1850s. The railway communities in remote locations were very tight, with their own schools, churches, and cemeteries. At the end of the nineteenth century Rudyard Kipling visited Jamalpur, which he described as being 'unadulteratedly "Railway"'. He went on to say that a visitor 'who has nothing to do with the E. I. Railway in some shape or another feels a stranger and an interloper'.[2] He wrote of the EIR being held in great reverence there, of how immaculate Jamalpur was, and how quiet when the 'thousands of natives and hundreds of Europeans'[3] were at work. As the railways grew, so did the number of its staff: across India by 1921 there were 18,000 British, European and Anglo-Indian railway employees. Anglo-Indians were fiercely loyal to the railways, keeping the BNR and EIR running during the respective strikes of 1927 and 1928.

Lists of railway employees are given in annual Bengal, Madras and Bombay directories and in *Thacker's Indian Directory*. By checking these it can be possible to trace the careers of those mentioned. For senior railway employees, particularly those of state railways, you should also consult the Civil lists in the *Army Lists* and the *India Office List* 1891–1947.

Railway officials could also have connections with other industries and it may be worth checking those records for further details. The writer and broadcaster Mark Tully was born in Calcutta in 1936. When travelling on the Darjeeling Himalayan railway to his boarding school in Darjeeling, he would tell his friends 'My father owns this railway', although his father was, in fact, a director. He writes, 'My father was a partner in a firm based in Kolkata, which managed not only the Darjeeling Himalayan Railway but a variety of companies, ranging from coal mines to construction, from insurance to jute manufacturing.'[4] For more on this railway see the website of the Darjeeling Himalayan Railway Society: http://www.dhrs.org.

Indian Railway Companies

In order to trace the career of your railway ancestor, you first need to identify which company or companies employed him. As railways were

PTE: GUNTHER, R.L.

D. O. No. 3624.

GOVERNMENT HOUSE,

CALCUTTA.

28th November 1937.

DEAR MAJOR HUMPHRIES,

His Excellency has already written to General Lindsay expressing his gratitude for the arrangements made by the Military Authorities in connection with his Public Arrival yesterday.

Lord Brabourne, however, wishes me to send you a special word of thanks for the Guard of Honour mounted by the Bengal-Nagpur Railway Regiment at Howrah Station, and he would like his appreciation conveyed to each officer and man who paraded with the Guard of Honour.

Yours sincerely,

R. B. BUTLER.

Major J. Humphries, E. D.,
Commanding, The Bengal-Nagpur Railway Regiment.

Letter from R.B. Butler, Government House, Calcutta to Major J. Humphries, Commanding The Bengal-Nagpur Railway Regiment, copied to Pte. R.L. Gunther (1937–11–02).
(Noel Gunther)

often amalgamated or their names changed, it is useful to check a history of the company in order to ascertain its names during the period in which your ancestor was employed. It is also important to note whether the company was private or was state-owned. Annual guides such as *Bradshaw's Railway Manual, Shareholders' Guide and Directory* (1854–1923) provide detailed information on railway companies, although you may need to search several editions as each company was not mentioned in every edition. Information on the railways of Australia, Canada, New Zealand, South Africa and the USA as well as India can be found in the annual *The Railway Book*, which ran from 1898 to 1932. This can be useful if your railway ancestor left India to work elsewhere.

Once you know which companies you would like to research, you can establish where their records are located. To discover more about the railway company that employed your ancestor, including the name of its successor, see the Railways section of the FIBIwiki site http://wiki.fibis.org/index.php?title=Category:Railways.

A distinction should be made between the names of railways and the names of the operating system that ran them. There were too many railways in India between 1853 and 1947 to examine in detail here but a complete run can be found in Hugh Wilding's excellent FIBIS Fact File No. 4: *Research sources for Indian Railways, 1845–1947*.

Changes in the companies and their routes in the 1920s and 1930s can be traced through the Indian Railway Conference Association (IRCA) railway route maps. Other railway maps can be found on the FIBIS website.

The railway companies which operated up to 1947 (with codes) were:

Assam-Bengal Railway (ABR)
Ahmadpur-Katwa Railway (AKR)
Assam Railways & Trading Company (ARTC/AR & TCR)
Arrah-Sasaram Light Railway (ASLR)
Bengal & Assam Railway (B & AR)
Bengal & North Western Railway (B & NWR)
Bombay Baroda & Central India Railway (BB & CIR)
Bankura Damodar (River) Railway (BDR/BDRR)
Bhavnagar-Gondal-Junagad-Porbandar Railway (BGJPR)
Bukhtiapur-Bihar Light Railway (BLR)
Bengal Nagpur Railway (BNR)
Bengal Provincial Railway (BPR)
Burma Railway (BR)

Barasat-Basirhat Light Railway (BBLR)
Bhavnagar State Railway (BSR)
Cutch State Railway (CSR)
Dholpur-Bari Light Railway (DBLR)
Darjeeling-Himalayan Railway (DHR)
Deoghur Railway (DR)
Dholpur-Bari Light Railway (DBLR)
Dibru-Sadiya Railway (DSR)
Eastern Bengal Railway (EBR)
East Indian Railway (EIR)
Futwah-Islampur Light Railway (FILR)
Gaekwar's Baroda State Railway (GBSR)
Great Indian Peninsula Railway (GIPR)
Gwalior Light Railway (GLR)
Gondal Railway (GR)
Howrah-Amta Light Railway (HALR)
Howrah-Sheakhalla Light Railway (HSLR)
Jodhpur-Bikaner Railway (JBR)
Jodhpur Railway (JR)
Jessore-Jhenidah Railway (JJR)
Junagad State Railway (JSR)
Kalighat-Falta Railway (KFR)
Madras Railway (MR)
Morvi-Rajkot-Wadhwan Railway (MRWR)
Mysore Railway (MSR)
Madras and Southern Mahratta Railway (M & SMR)
Nizam's Guaranteed Railway (NGR)
Nizam's State Railway (NSR)
North-Western Railway (NWR)
Oudh & Rohilkhand Railway (O & RR)
Oudh & Tirhut Railway (O & TR)
Porbander State Railway (PSR)
Rohilkhand & Kumaon Railway (R & KR/RKR)
South Indian Railways (SIR)
Southern Mahratta Railway (SMR)
Scinde, Punjab & Delhi Railway (SP & DR)
Southern Punjab Railway (SPR)
Shahdara-Saharanpur Light Railway (SSLR)
Tezpore-Balipara Light Railway (TBLR)
Udaipur-Chitor Railway (UCR)

Railway records: staff
Most records of staff remained with the respective railway company or its sucessor. You can access them by contacting the company directly, although some may require a reference. Do be aware that several companies have merged with others or have changed their names. You are also more likely to find records of white-collar railway staff than of the 'navvies' that helped build the first railways. However, if your ancestor rose through the ranks you may be successful in finding details of their later career in these records.

Towards the end of the nineteenth century locomotives began to be built in India, and railway workers were now being trained there to a high standard. Thus, by the twentieth century, recruitment from Britain was rare.

The British Library holds a number of staff records for state and private railways in the India Office Records collection. Many but not all of the staff found in these were appointed in the UK. These records are located mainly in the L and V series.

State Railways

Indian State Railways were those owned and managed by the Indian Government. If you think your ancestor may have been appointed to these railways in the UK, or you are unsure, begin your research by checking the Z/L/F/8/1–2 index to the records of appointments to State Railways made in the UK 1855–1946 (L/F/8/1–20) on the open-access shelves. Do note that this list is not comprehensive and does not include all railway workers who were appointed in the UK 1855–1946. If you find your ancestor named here you can follow up the reference given by ordering the stated document.

If you have not found your ancestor in this index, you may find him in one of the following records which include employees appointed in the UK and also in India. Half-yearly pay lists are particularly useful for tracing a railwayman's career:

Histories of Service, 1884–1953 in V/12/51–52, 54–62 & 66–80: these include railwaymen who earned more than 1,000 rupees per month.

Civil Lists, Public Works Department 1861–1904 in V/13/195–213: names of officers and workmen of State Railways only.

Civil Lists, Railway Board, Department and Ministry 1905–57 in V/13/227–43: officers and workmen of State Railways and officers of privately-managed railways.

BOARD OF APPRENTICESHIP TRAINING.

APPRENTICESHIP ADMISSION EXAMINATION – January, 1935.

The names of the over-age candidates who passed the Board of Apprenticeship Training Admission Examination held in January 1935 are given below :-

In order of merit.

First Class.–	Roll No.	N a m e s.
1.	126	Subodh Chandra Ray.
2	120	Robert Lionel Gunther.
Second Class.–		
3	53	Arthur Reginald Oliviere.
4	119	Austin Owen Gunther.
5	6	Ram Kumar Banerjee.
6	100	Nani Gopal Chakrabarty.
7	94	Shankar Das.
8	138	Kesheo Madheo Tikekar.
9	5	James Derrick Stuart.
10	115	Anant Kesheo Vyas.
11	117	Nirmalendu Ganguli.
12	127	Sambhu Nath Chatterjee.
13	3	Romendra Nath Gupta.

E. J. Hoghen

5/2/35

Dated, Calcutta,

The 5th Feb. 1935.

Secretary,

Board of Apprenticeship Training.

Memo No. AT-5/787-821.   Dated 18th Feb. 1935.

Apprenticeship Admission Examination 1935. List and Class of Candidates. (Noel Gunther)

Lists of State Railway employees 1884–1900 in L/F/10/229–44.

Half-yearly lists of officers of the Burma Railway Company 1922–28 in L/F/10/250.

Annual lists of Covenanted Railway Employees 1927–36 & 1937–47 in L/SG/6/64 & 860.

Railway Companies

If you do not find your ancestor in any of the State Railway records, you should check the *IOR Lists 205 Index to Names in L/AG/46 UK Appointments to Indian Railways 1849–1925*. If you find your ancestor's name here, you can follow up the reference in *Agreements with employees 1881–1925 and index to appointments made in the UK 1848–80* in L/AG/46/12/86–88.

Other useful records for the staff of private companies are as follows:

Bengal Central Railway Company List of Employees 1886–96 in L/AG/46/4/11.

Burma Railway Company List of Employees 1898–1921 in L/AG/46/6/17–18.

Calcutta and South-East Railway Company Staff appointments made from UK 1856–66 in L/AG/46/4/13.

East India Railway Company Staff appointments made from UK 1858–1925 in L/AG/46/11/133–137.

Eastern Bengal Railway Company Staff appointments made from UK 1862–69, and lists of staff 1879–81 in L/AG/46/10/35.

EIR alphabetical list of Europeans &c in service in ORB 30/4772.

EIR Half-yearly Lists of Staff 1861–1890 and 1911–22 in L/AG/46/11/138–141 give ages of staff after 1886.

Great Indian Peninsula Railway Company Staff appointments made from UK 1881–1925 in L/AG/46/12/86–88.

GIPR Staff files 1901–1955 in L/S & G/11.

Madras Railway shareholder declarations of identity, certified copies of marriages & burials 1857–1908 in L/AG/46/15/26–42.

Sind (Punjab, Delhi) Railway Company Lists of Staff 1868–69 in L/AG/46/17/12.

South Indian Railway Company Staff appointments made from UK 1891– 1940 in L/AG/466/18/1–4.

James St Clair Burns. James St Clair Burns was an Inspector with the East Indian Railway (EIR) in its very early years. We know from his marriage record that he married at Dinapore on 7 December 1855, allegedly aged 20, and that his father was Timothy Burns.

He was listed in the *New Calcutta Directory 1856 parts 6–10* (p. 93 List of Mofussil Inhabitants) under *Burns, J St. Clair – Monghyr, inspector of east indian railway co.*; in the *New Calcutta Directory 1857* (p. 256 List of Mofussil Inhabitants) as *Burns, J St. Clair – Monghyr, inspector of east indian railway co.* but not found after that date – significantly, after the Mutiny.

James was mentioned in the staff lists for 1862 and 1864 in *The Early History of The East India Railway 1845–1879* by Hena Mukherjee.[5]

Unfortunately it is not clear whether he inspected the railways, the trains or the tickets. If he were a ticket-inspector he may have been employed in India and served originally in the Army there. (However, he was not found in the *Index to names in UK appointments to India Railways 1849–1925* (ref. L/AG/46).)

Other Sources for Tracing Railway Ancestors

Within India itself there are records of the Railway Board (1905–47) held at NAI.

Monthly staff magazines contain information on railway ancestors that you are unlikely to find elsewhere. The house journal for the Eastern Bengal Railway 1928–33 can be found at the British Library in SV 608/ 1–6; the house journal for the EIR 1928–33 is in SV 492/1–6; the house journal for the Indian State Railways 1927–38 in SV 14/1–11. Sadly they are not indexed but they are worth searching through in order to find out about the life your ancestor led as well as for trying to find his name or image. Other staff magazines that are not held at the British Library are the *Bengal Nagpur Railway Magazine*, *GIP Railway Magazine* and *North Western Railway Magazine*. Archives which hold these and other staff magazines can be located through searching on the name of the railway company at www.copac.ac.uk. This tells us that, for example, a copy of the *GIP Railway Magazine* for 1924 is held at the National Railway Museum in York (www.nrm.org.uk).

Railway journals contain obituaries and other reports of railway ancestors in railway-specific publications such as the *Indian Railway Gazette, The Railway Gazette, The Railway Magazine* and *The Railway Engineer*.

Other occupational journals may mention ancestors in the relevant trades of *The Builder, The Engineer, Engineering, The English Mechanic* and *Mechanics Magazine*.

Professional organizations hold for their well-qualified staff various educational records (see Chapter 7). The British Library holds calendars of names of those students at the Royal Indian Engineering College (RIEC) 1873–1903 (V/25/700/1–25); as some of these students had previously attended Haileybury, it is worth checking its records also. A detailed introduction to the College and its records can be found on the open-access shelves in L/PWD/8 (formerly K/3). Indian State Railway Candidates 1914–*c*1920 can be found in L/PWD/8/408. General railway records are in V/25/720, including some names and histories of railway projects 1899–1906. There are some education records in V/25/860–867. The RIEC was based at Cooper's Hill, Egham, Surrey and is more commonly referred to as 'Cooper's Hill College'. Besides railway engineers, the college also trained public works engineers and, from 1883, forestry officers.

Many went on to be members of either the Institution of Civil Engineers (ICE) or the Institution of Mechanical Engineers (IMechE). Members' application forms (from 1818) survive at ICE, and career, residence and death information can be found by tracing your ancestor through the annual lists. More information can be found at the website www.ice.org.uk and abstracts of obituaries for some members can be seen via a name search on the virtual library at www.iceknowledge.com. IMechE also holds membership records (dating from 1847) and some records of the Institution of Locomotive Engineers (ILocoE) from 1911 but useful genealogical information is only found after 1875. A good collection of obituaries and career details is held and abstracted proposal forms 1847–1907 can be seen at the archive database http://62.173.95.116/dserve. For more details on the archive see http://www.imeche.org/knowledge/library/archive.

Biographical information can also be found on engineers in Bell's *A biographical index of British engineers in the 19th century* and Sharp's *Obituaries of British Engineers 1901–1920*. Details from Chrimes' *Biographical dictionary of civil engineers in Great Britain and Ireland Vol 2 (1830–1890)* of those who served in India can be searched on the FIBIS database at http://search.fibis.org/frontis/bin/aps_browse_sources.php?mode=browse_components&id=424&s_id=0.

132

Occupations given on Indian baptism, marriage or burial records – or in newspaper birth, marriage and death announcements – can help to trace a railway worker's career over time. This is useful for ancestors of all ranks.

Many of the railway staff in India had first worked on the railways in Britain. If you know your ancestor was employed here, check for railway records on them at TNA. For more details see TNA's Railway Workers Research Guide at http://www.nationalarchives.gov.uk/records/looking-for-person/railwayworker.htm. If your ancestor worked in England for the Southern Railway Company, you may find his name online in Bob Rubie's Southern Railway Magazine 1840–1942 database at http://search.ancestry.co.uk/search/db.aspx?dbid=4955.

Other useful information at TNA includes Board of Trade records for the railway companies (BT 41, BT 31 & BT 285), Retired Railway Officers' Society biographies 1900–63 in RAIL 1156/11–26, and the War Diary of the 2 Indian Railway Construction Battalion January–April 1918 in WO95/5246.

Check Access to Archives http://www.nationalarchives.gov.uk/a2a for holdings related to your ancestor or his railway in local record offices in the UK. Among surviving records related to Indian railway companies are personal letters, share dividends or private ledgers. SOAS has records of individuals who worked for Indian railways; as does the Centre of South Asian Studies at Cambridge which holds the diaries (1851–1863), notebooks and autobiography of the EIR engineer, George Turnbull.

You should also check the British Library catalogue, particularly for any private papers that survive, such as those of D.M. Roche, a Traffic Manager of the East Indian Railway, or the EIR staff photographs 1905–10, both of which are held in the MSS Eur series.

To see items in the UK relating to the history of railways, such as model carriages of the Bombay Baroda & Central India Railway, items of staff uniform and shields you can visit the National Railway Museum at York and Shildon. See http://www.nrm.org.uk/PlanaVisit.aspx for more details.

Further information on Indian railways can be found at the Indian Railways Fan Club Association site http://www.irfca.org.

A useful guide for general research into railway ancestors is Tom Richards' *Was your Grandfather a Railwayman?*

The railways of India: with an account of their rise, progress, and construction by Edward Davidson and Kipling's 'Among the Railway Folk' in *From*

Sea to Sea: Letters of Travel (Forgotten Books, 1899) can both be read in full on Google Books.

Notes

1. The Doctrine of Lapse referred to an annexation policy instigated by Dalhousie in 1848, whereby the princely states of rulers who had no natural heir, or were 'manifestly incompetent', would lapse to the control of the EIC. The policy was extremely unpopular with the Indian population, many of whom considered it unlawful.
2. Rudyard Kipling, 'Among the Railway Folk', in *From Sea to Sea: Letters of Travel*, p. 249.
3. Ibid., p. 252.
4. Mark Tully, *India's Unending Journey*, pp. 224–5.
5. Hena Mukherjee, *The Early History of The East India Railway 1845–1879*, pp. 108–9.

Chapter 9

PROBATE RECORDS

This is the last will and testament of me, Richard Heldar. I am in sound bodily and mental health, and there is no previous will to revoke.

Rudyard Kipling, 'The Light That Failed'
in *The Works of Rudyard Kipling.*

Probate records, such as wills, administrations and inventories, can be one of the most useful genealogical tools. Wills were written by the deceased before death in order to indicate his or her wishes for disposal of personal property and/or real estate. Other probate records were created after death but like wills, they can include names of relatives, residences and useful dates. Many of your ancestor's probate records may be found in the UK. However, for British and European ancestors who lived in India, these documents are often found within the IOR. Records of non-Europeans are also sometimes included, particularly after 1860, and these are being digitized on Find My Past.

These records can include the name and address of the deceased, names of beneficiaries, and names of executors. Other probate records of British ancestors who lived in South Asia may be found in relevant small archives across Britain, as well as at major repositories like TNA and the Principal Probate Registry in central London.

Probate of Those with Property in India

Probate records in the IOR (British Library)
To begin the search for a probate record you need to have some idea of when and where your ancestor died, and ideally, where he or she lived. You should be able to find this out through vital records or employment details. However, as a probate record can help you discover the exact date of death it is worth exploring the indexes, even if you only have a

rough idea of when your ancestor died. Probate records include wills, grants of administrations (admons), and inventories for wills that have been proved in a court. Admons were issued in cases of intestacy or where there was no (available) executor.

Wills and admons can be useful to the genealogist where they name family members, or simply where they summarize the wealth of your ancestor, name executors and witnesses, and give the date of death. In wills you may also find evidence of a second family, a mistress or native woman with whom your male British ancestor had children. In *Poor Relations*, C.J. Hawes reveals that by 1830, one out of six wills mentioned a native companion. On the other hand, inventories containing details of your ancestor's possessions – such as clothes and furniture – can contribute to understanding who your ancestor was and what kind of a life he or she led.

Probate everywhere is a complex legal process but finding the correct record in the IOR can be difficult. Fortunately, most of the records are indexed. The main series of wills, probates and administrations runs from 1727 to 1948. The largest collection of probate records is found within the records of the Accountant General, organized under the L/AG/34 reference.

Indexes

As probate did not always occur in the same year as death, it is sensible to check up to five years afterwards for when the grant or will was proved. Some wills were proved up to twenty years after the decease. Even if you know where your ancestor died, check the indexes of all three Presidencies as property may have been held elsewhere. Where you do not find your ancestor in the index, remember that not every will is recorded in these records, even if one was written.

Early records may be found in the Mayor's Court Proceedings (IOR series P). Indexes to Inventories in the Mayor's Court Calcutta Proceedings can be found in Z/L/AG/34/3, and those of Madras Inventories 1753–79 are in Z/L/AG/34/3.

The main series of documents, which date from 1773, is indexed on open shelves AAS in *IOR Lists 203a–m, volumes 1–8*. Copies of some of these indexes can also be found in LDS History Centres (www.family search.org) and on the FIBIS website (http://wiki.fibis.org/index.php?title=Wills,_Administrations,_Probate_and_Inventories). The FIBIS database includes complete indexes of Bengal wills from 1780 to 1866; from 1867–1909 transcriptions are for surnames beginning with 'A' only.

Another list of Officers' Wills provides an index and extract from the IOR series L/AG/34/30/30. This includes the wills of thirty-seven officers from all three Presidencies over the years 1831 to 1875.

Volume 1, General Indexes to Admons, Wills & Inventories of Deceased Estates in Bengal, Madras and Bombay 1704–83 (Z/L/AG/34/1–2; Z/L/AG/34/3).

Volume 2, Indexes to Admons Bengal 1774–1909 (Z/L/AG/34/4–5).

Volume 3, Indexes to Wills Bengal 1780–1909 (Z/L/AG/34/6–7).

Volume 4, Indexes to Inventories Bengal 1780–1948 (Z/L/AG.34/13–14; includes Bihar Inventories 1919–44).

Volume 5, Indexes to Admons, Wills & Inventories of Deceased Estates Madras 1780–1909 (Z/L/AG/34/8; Z/L/AG/34/9; Z/L/AG/34/15).

Volume 6, Indexes to Admons, Wills & Inventories of Deceased Estates Bombay 1776–1909 (Z/L/AG/34/10; Z/L/AG/34/16 – all that survives for 1778–98 are records of delivery of inventories to the Mayor's Court).

Volume 7, Indexes to Probate and Administrations granted by District Courts in India 1865–1910.

Volume 8, Index to Wills, Probates, Administrations and Inventories of Deceased Estates 1909–48 (parts 1–5; A–Z).

Probate pre-1727

Before 1727 testamentary jurisdiction for the British in India was exercised informally in the three Presidencies by the Governor and Council in Bengal, the Court of Admiralty in Madras, and the Court of Judicature in Bombay. For this early period, the IOR holds a volume of early wills 1618–1725 for Persia, India and South-East Asia (ref. G/40/23). Bengal wills 1704–27 are recorded in the Bengal Public/Court Proceedings (ref. P/1/1–6).

In 1726 a Royal Charter Act allowed British courts to recognize the East India Company's Courts' jurisdiction over testamentary and intestate matters. From 1727/28, powers of probate were issued from the Mayor's Courts in the three Presidencies of Bengal, Madras and Bombay.

Mayor's Court Proceedings 1727–83 (series P):

P/154/61–70 (M); P/155/1–8 (M) Inventories in the Mayor's Court Calcutta Proceedings.

P/328/60–64 (M) Madras Inventories 1753–79.

P/1/1–6 (M); P/154/40–60 Bengal Wills & Administrations 1704–79.

(M 47–49 are missing)

P/155/9–38 (M); P/155/53–59 (M).

P/416/77–98 (M) Bombay Wills & Administrations 1728–83.

P/328/60–64(M); P/328/71–79 Madras Wills & Administrations 1736–79.

(M), G/18/6–7.

R/9/11–13 (M) Malacca wills and estate papers 1685–1827.

After the Regulating Act of 1773, the Calcutta Mayor's Court was replaced by the Calcutta Supreme Court (1774–1862); and the Madras and Bombay Mayors' Courts were replaced by Recorders' Courts. In 1862 High Courts (1862–1938) in Bengal, Madras and Bombay replaced these Supreme Courts. Later, in 1866, a High Court was established in Allahabad, and a Chief Court was created in the Punjab. Burma's Chief Court was created in 1900.

For probate records after 1773 you need to consult the records of the official agent to the Administrator General in India and the records of the Estates and Wills Branch in L/AG/34.

Accountant General's Records British India and Burma 1774–1948

This series includes wills, probates, administrations and inventories of estates of persons who died in India and Burma.

The first record of an appointment as Official Agent to the Administrators General was in 1851, when the office was joined with that of Clerk in Charge of Ecclesiastical Registration. From this date, it is believed that the Administrators General also began to oversee the administration in England of the estates and wills of persons dying in India.

When consulting the military series it is important to note that soldiers' wills were often written at the point of death, and, although often just immediate personal effects are listed, some do give names and addresses of relatives in the UK. L/AG/34/30, volumes 1–29 cover only European other ranks of the EIC/Indian Army. In some cases a soldier's will may also be recorded in the Treasury Deposits series (L/AG/34/33), the general series of wills (L/AG/34/29) and the Military Estate Papers (L/AG/34/40; L/AG/29/1/210–261).

Estates of Deceased Soldiers/Treasury Deposits are half-yearly, quarterly and monthly returns to the UK of the estates of European officers/other ranks of the EIC/Indian Army; see Treasury Deposits' indexes Z/L/AG/34/17–21. These refer to European officers and other ranks of the EIC/Indian Army. Though less informative than the Military Estate Papers, they give name of the deceased, rank and unit, date of death, amount of money left in Indian rupees and sterling equivalent, plus name and address of next-of-kin.

Military Estate Papers contain inventories for soldiers serving in the East India Company Armies and the Indian Army. The papers are indexed:

L/AG/34/1: Correspondence from the Administrators General.

L/AG/34/2: Registers of Miscellaneous Letters from Administrators General and of Consequential Letters to Persons Outside India.

L/AG/34/3: Copies of Letters from Administrators General to Solicitors and Others in the UK.

L/AG/34/4: References to the Official Agent from Other Departments of India Office.

L/AG/34/5: References from the Official Agent to Other Departments.

L/AG/34/6: Returns of Moneys Received in India by Administrators General in Respect of Deceased Estates.

L/AG/34/7: Advices from Administrators General of Amounts Paid into Treasuries for Remittance of the Official Agent.

L/AG/34/8: Ledger Accounts Maintained by the Official Agent of Estates Disbursed by Him.

L/AG/34/9: Lawford Papers: home & overseas correspondence of Messrs Lawford & Waterhouse, Solicitors who acted for the EIC and the IO (Indian estates which caused difficulty legally).

L/AG/34/10: Quarterly Accounts of Official Agent with Administrators General in India and with the Cashier.

L/AG/34/11: Summaries of Unpaid Remittances.

L/AG/34/12: Declarations made by Claimants before Payment of the Amount of Certain Estates.

L/AG/34/13: Register of Probates Lodged at the India Office in connection with Payment of balances of estates which has been reformed by Administrators General 1903–1938.

L/AG/34/14: Indexes of Estates Advertised by Administrators General & Others.

L/AG/34/14A: Returns of Deaths of Uncovenanted Servants and Other Officers 1870–1949.

L/AG/34/15: Miscellany Book of the Official Agent's Department 1858–1886.

L/AG/34/16: Miscellaneous Returns & Statements received from India.

L/AG/34/17: Home Correspondence of the Estates & Will Branch 1852–1909.

L/AG/34/18: Registers of Home Correspondence of the Combined Sections.

L/AG/34/19: Copies of Outward Letters from the Department, mainly Home Correspondence.

L/AG/34/20: Register of Letters from India.

L/AG/34/21: Letters from India enclosing Ecclesiastical Returns, Wills & Inventories.

L/AG/34/22: Miscellaneous Home Registers & Returns: Military Effects Books.

L/AG/34/23: Register of Deceased Estates Escheated to the East India Company or the Crown.

L/AG/34/24: Deceased Military Estates 1867–1947.

L/AG/34/25: Disposal of Articles of Effects.

L/AG/34/26A: Copy of the *London Gazette* giving lists of Unclaimed Estates in the custody of the Supreme Court of Judicature in London 2 March 1889.

L/AG/34/26B: Specimens of printed forms used in the estates and wills branch, with particular reference to the estates of deceased military personnel.

L/AG/34/26C: Index to the records of the estates of and wills and official agency branch 1912.

L/AG/34/27: Inventories & Accounts of Deceased Estates – Bengal, Madras & Bombay (1778–1938).

L/AG/34/27/1–252: Bengal Inventories.

L/AG/34/27/253–386: Madras Inventories (1780–1821 Madras Inventories are to be found with the Madras Wills 1780–1821).

L/AG/34/27/387–425: Bombay Inventories & Accounts of Deceased Estates (1798–1937).

L/AG/34/28 (M): Inventories & Accounts of Deceased Estates – Straits Settlements, Prince of Wales Island, Singapore and Malacca 1819–1929.

L/AG/34/29: Accountant General's Records British India & Burma 1774–1948: this series includes wills, probates, administrations & inventories of estates of persons who died in India & Burma.

L/AG/34/29/1–184 (4–182 M): Bengal Wills & (from April 1836) Administrations (1774–1938).

L/AG/34/29/185–340 (M): Madras Wills & Administrations (1780–1938).

L/AG/34/29/290–300 (M): Asian Wills & administrations in Northern India 1890–1900 (index in Z/L/AG/34/11).

L/AG/34/29/341–380 (341–378 M): Bombay Wills & Administrations (1783–1937).

L/AG/34/29/382: Burma Probates & Administrations (1937–1947).

L/AG/34/29/383–386: All India Wills & Administrations 1938–1948 (covers the High Courts & District Courts). This series mainly covers probates and administrations only (although there are some wills & inventories from Bihar 1938–1944).

L/AG/34/30: Soldiers Wills 1820–1881.

L/AG/34/30/1–12: Bengal Soldiers Wills (1825–1867; nos 170–230 in Vol. 9 are Madras wills).

L/AG/34/30/13–22: Madras Soldiers Wills (1825–1881).

L/AG/34/30/23–29: Bombay Soldiers Wills (1825–1868).

L/AG/34/30/30: Bengal, Madras & Bombay Officers' Wills (April 1831–July 1875).

L/AG/34/31: Probates & Administrations Granted by District Courts in India 1865–1938. District Probates are grants of probate & administrations only (except there are full copies of Lower Burma wills from 1898 to 1918; some 1919–1921; full copies of Bihar wills & inventories 1919–38).

L/AG/34/31/1–21 (4–21 M): District Courts Probates & Administrations.

L/AG/34/32/1–3: Straits Settlements wills, accounts etc. 1806–1853 (M).

L/AG/34/33: Estates of Deceased Soldiers/Treasury Deposits 1792–1927.

L/AG/34/33/1–63: Bengal.

L/AG/34/33/12–19: Madras.

L/AG/34/33/22–25: Bombay.

L/AG/34/40: Military Estate Papers 1849–1937.

L/AG/34/40/1–104: Bengal & India.

L/AG/34/40/105–137: Madras.

L/AG/34/40/138–144: Bombay.

L/AG/34/40/145–156: India (Duplicates 1919–1937).

Ordering Probate Records in the British Library

Many of the records listed above need to be ordered via Explore theBritishLibrary at http://explore.bl.uk. Probate records, like others in the IOR, need to be ordered by clicking on the Request list tab. Click on the option for 'Asia, Pacific and Africa Collections' and then 'India Office Records'. The L/AG reference can then be entered.

Where you find your ancestor's name in the name indexes listed above, you should then note the year of probate, whether there was a will/admon/inventory, and also the L/AG reference on the spine of the volume's index. Using the L/AG reference you have noted, check the spine of the index you have just consulted for the reference. Next you need to look at the relevant binder for the document and year you are researching and look for the year you have noted. The L/AG/34 reference for that year will be the reference you need to order.

For example, once you have found a name in the index, note the year – for example, 1780 – and whether an Administration, Will or Inventory. When ordering an Administration from Bengal in 1780, you would find L/AG/34/29/1–154 on the spine of the index. Collect the L/AG/34 binder part III (L/AG/34–52) and find the correct year for the Bengal Administrations; for 1780, you will need L/AG/34/29/1 which covers 1774–99.

The will of Joseph Richardson, Bengal Branch Pilot. Among the IOR probate records are a very detailed will and an inventory (deceased estate) for Joseph Richardson, who resided in Calcutta and died on 2 April 1840. The Inventory is held in L/AG/34/27/121, part 3, on pages 348–50 and provides an interesting list of items owned by Joseph Richardson at the time of death.

The Will from 1840 Bengal Wills (ref. L/AG/34/29/62, part 2, pages 121–6) however, is more useful genealogically, as it gives detailed information on Joseph's relatives. The will tells us, for example, that Joseph wished to be buried 'with my beloved wife Mary Richardson'. It continues to name other relatives – some deceased – and provide details of residences:

> … to my daughter Mary Isabella Richardson the silver teapot, presented to me by Lady William Bentick, my mourning locket brooch containing her late dear mother's hair with a record of her death all my silver plate bearing the initials JMR all her late dear mother's Jewelry [*sic*] (including her wedding ring her wearing apparel toilet glass and toilet table) also the PianoForte I purchased for her and the miniatures of my father and mother.
>
> To my son Joseph William Richardson … gold double cased watch … my gold brooch … I also forgive him all monies that he may owe to me at the time of my demise …
>
> Son, James Richardson … silver mug bequeathed by Mr William Birch … double cased silver watch (presented by father, William Richardson) … gold seal ring my crest having my crest and initials engraved on a blood stone and my long Dollands spy glass …
>
> Son, Daniel Richardson … gold snuff box presented to me by the Honorable Mrs Holanburgh as a particular mark of my affection for [Daniel's] very kind and dutiful conduct towards his dear mother

during her last illness also as a mark of my approbation of his general good conduct ...

Should I not succeed in getting a situation for my son Charles Bertody Richardson previous to my demise I will that the sum of [...] be paid to him for his support for twelve months from the day of my death and no longer ...

Beloved sister Mrs Isabella Bahana of No 12 upper Copenhagen Street White Conduit Fields Islington London ...

My mother in law Mrs Frederica Witchlowe of Calcutta the sum of Company's Rupees 200 ...

My upper roomed house situated in Pudderpooler Entaly ... to be sold.

Probate of Those with Property outside India

Many people who died in India had their wills resealed in Britain. Others had wills or admons proved in Britain as they held property there also. A number of Britons intended to work and live in India for a short time only but sadly died before they could return to their families, homes and business interests back home. Some sailors who died at sea in the India area had their wills proved in Britain, as did several senior officials of the EIC.

Pre-1858 England & Wales
Before 1858 the probate of many British people was granted in various courts across the land, and is thus held in various archives today. Some ancestors may have had wills proved at more than one of these courts. However, most wills of richer English and Welsh ancestors are to be found in the Prerogative Court of Canterbury (PCC) records, which are indexed on TNA's website www.nationalarchives.gov.uk/documents online. Several maritime and military ancestors are also found in these records.

Other wills proved in England or Wales before 1858 may be found at the National Wills Index http://www.nationalwillsindex.com and http://www.origins.net.

A number of probate records have been indexed on www.findmypast. co.uk: Probate and Wills Records Collection 1462–1858, including the Bank of England Wills Extracts Index 1717–1845, London Probate Index 1750–1858, Northamptonshire and Rutland Probate Index 1462–1857, PCC Wills 1750–1800, Suffolk Testator and Beneficiary Indices 1847–57, and the West Kent Probate Index 1750–1858.

The Corporation of London's London Signatures index that included 10,000 Archdeaconry Court of Middlesex Wills 1609–1810 and 23,500 Diocese of Winchester records have now been digitized on www.ancestry. co.uk. The Extracted Probate Records (see http://search.ancestry.co.uk/ search/db.aspx?dbid=1610) include records from a number of areas across the UK, including Scotland.

The Diocese of London Consistory Court Wills index is online at http://217.154.230.218/NR/rdonlyres/17B65CB7-D22C-468D-9EE9-DE22B646C762/0/WillsAB.pdf and at the London Metropolitan Archives. These records are now included in Ancestry's London, England, Wills and Probate, 1525–1858 at http://search.ancestry.co.uk/search/db.aspx? dbid=1704, along with records of the London Commissary Court, the Peculiar Court of the Dean and Chapter of St Paul's, and the Archdeaconry Court of Surrey. Full details on London, Middlesex and Surrey wills can be found at http://217.154.230.218/NR/rdonlyres/2FDBO1F7-C781-44D5-A492-61EE38E88A94/0/6/WILLSFORLONDON.pdf.

www.thegenealogist.co.uk holds the Bristol Wills Index, the Leicestershire Wills Index, the Northampton Wills Index, the PCC Wills Index and the Yorkshire Wills Index.

Wills proved at the lower Welsh ecclesiastical courts can be found at the National Library of Wales. The Library's guide to wills and probate can be seen online at http://www.llgc.org.uk/index.php?id=487.

Pre-1858 probate records for Durham can be searched online at http://familyrecords.dur.ac.uk/nei/data/intro.php.

Wiltshire wills can be searched at http://history.wiltshire.gov.uk/heritage.

Wills of Royal Naval Seamen 1786–1882 held at TNA in ADM 48 have been digitized at http://www.nationalarchives.gov.uk/documentsonline/willsdeathduties.asp. Further wills can be searched up to 1909 via Digital Microfilm. Pieces ADM 142/1–14 provide the name, address and relationship of the executor or administrator of the will, which supplement the wills themselves.

Royal Marine wills and administrations can be found in ADM 96/524 (1740–64). Wills deposited in the Navy pay office by Royal Marines other ranks (1786–1909) are indexed in ADM 142. There may also be copy wills in the series PROB 11. The PCC was responsible for proving the wills of naval officers and ratings that died with more than £20 of wages due to them. You can search the PROB 11 wills in DocumentsOnline.

For sailors who enlisted after 1882 the National Probate Index of the Principal Probate Registry should be consulted. Further probate information can be found in original documents held at TNA: Officers' effects papers in series ADM 45 and Seamen's effects papers in ADM 44. There is also a register of probates affecting the payment of pensions in PMG 50 (1836–1915).

FIBIS holds very useful probate information for this period including PCC indexes, some of which do not feature on TNA's site (such as records of PCC Administrations from 1384 to 1858). FIBIS also has details of the Administrations relating to India 1830–39 and 1840–57.

Post-1858 England & Wales
Civil Probate was introduced in England and Wales on 11 January 1858. From then on English and Welsh wills and admons were proved by the Probate Service, part of the Family Division of the High Court. Records from 1861 to 1941 are now indexed on www.ancestry.co.uk in the England & Wales National Probate Calendar 1861–1941. However, copies of the original grants, wills and admons need to be ordered from the Probate Service itself; a guide to obtaining probate records can be seen online at http://www.hmcourts-service.gov.uk/cms/1176.htm. The Principal Probate Registry (PPR) in High Holborn, London holds bound volumes for each year up to the 1990s, and also houses an incomplete computer index for probate records from 1920 (Willfinder) and a complete computerized index for all records from 1996 (Probate-man). These can be searched in person at the Registry and copies of wills and admons ordered there for £5 each. PPR is only a short walk from the British Library.

Some LDS Family History Centres hold microfilm copies of India Calendars of probate 1865 1936, listing grants of probates or administrations made on the estates of all persons of European extraction by the District Courts. See www.familysearch.org for further details.

For further details on probate and the complicated court system in England and Wales before 1858 see *Wills and Probate Records* (2nd Edition), Karen Grannum and Nigel Taylor.

Scotland
Probate law in Scotland was administered differently from that in England and Wales. From the sixteenth century, probate was granted at Commissary Courts until these were abolished in 1823. Subsequently, testaments (grants of probate) were confirmed at the Sheriff Courts. In Scotland all heritable property (land, buildings, mines etc) was passed to the eldest son by rule of primogeniture unless the deceased formally noted it otherwise. Relatively fewer Scots left wills but for those that did, the ScotlandsPeople site has a free index to wills and testaments

1513–1901 at http://www.scotlandspeople.gov.uk/content/help/index. aspx?r=554&407. For a fee, images of the wills and testaments can also be seen. The original documents are held at the National Archives of Scotland (NAS) but have been withdrawn from use.

The Edinburgh Wills Index can be seen at www.thegenealogist.co.uk.

However, wills from 1902 can be ordered at NAS after searching for the deceased in the Calendar of Confirmations. For 1985–1996, the calendar is computerized in the search room. For further details, see http://www. nas.gov.uk/guides/wills.asp.

Ireland

Irish Origins holds several indexes to probate material including the Irish Wills Index 1484–1858, the Dublin Will & Grant Books Index 1270–1858, the Phillimore & Thrift Indexes to Irish Wills 1536–1858, and the Vicars' Index to the Prerogative Wills of Ireland 1536–1810.

The Index to the Will Calendar Entries for the District Probate Registries of Armagh, Belfast and Londonderry 1858–1919 and 1922–1943 can be found at the website of the Public Record Office of Northern Ireland www.proni.gov.uk.

www.familyrelatives.com holds a good collection of Irish probate records, including the Index to Prerogative Wills of Ireland 1536–1810 and the Quaker Records Dublin Abstracts of Wills. As well as names, addresses and dates, these abstracts feature relatives, occupations, witnesses, freeholds, monies and inventories. This website also holds Indexes to Irish Wills 1536–1857 (5 Volumes), plus the Irish Genealogical Guide copies and Abstracts of Irish Wills 1445 to 1834.

An Index to Irish Wills Volumes 1 & 2 appears on www.ancestry.co.uk as part of the Irish Records Index 1500–1920. These records were donated to the government after the 1922 fire at the Public Record Office in Dublin. They have subsequently been microfilmed by the LDS and the full copies can be found at the Family History Library in Utah. The index details include names, dates of probate and residences.

www.ancestry.co.uk also houses the Irish Records Extraction Database 1600–1874, which includes abstracts of around 1,000 wills from Ireland taken from Wallace Clare's *Irish Genealogical Guides: a Guide to Copies & Abstracts of Irish Wills (First Series), Volume 1.*

The Irish Wills Index can also be found at www.thegenealogist.co.uk.

Chapter 10

INDIAN INDEPENDENCE AND LIFE AFTER 1947

I shall be the last Englishman to rule India.

Jawaharlal Nehru,
quoted in J.K. Galbraith,
A Life in Our Times (1981)

History of the Indian Independence Movement

Animosity against British rule and calls for independence grew stronger and louder in the early part of the twentieth century. The high-caste Hindu-dominated Indian National Congress and the Muslim League began organizing a united nationalism movement against the British Government. Britain, in contrast, still needed India for strategic purposes and for its significance to the Empire. There were economic considerations too: British goods were sold to India, Britain needed Indian gold, and India remained in debt to Britain. Before the Great War it was thus inconceivable to many Britons that the British would ever leave India.

What we know of as the *Raj* was at its height in this era, with the Viceroys and British upper classes living sometimes luxurious lives as shown by the example of the Curzons (see pp. 55–56). However, life for lower-class Britons on the *cantonments* was often far from pleasant and fatal illnesses still struck with regularity. Surprisingly, *Raj* was not a term that most Europeans tended to use as the British were not the only rulers in India; most tended to use 'the Empire' or 'the Indian empire' instead.

Britain's declaration of war against Germany in 1914 brought the independence movement into focus. Like other countries across the Empire, India was swiftly instructed that she was at war and was asked to commit troops for the Allied campaign. Indians volunteered in their thousands, contributing greatly to the war effort. As a result, 64,449 Indians are believed to have died; 13,000 members of Indian Corps won gallantry medals, including twelve Victoria crosses. In return, Indians expected more rights from their rulers. Many Muslims were also angered by having fought against fellow Muslims, who were among the troops of the Ottoman Empire. Feeling betrayed, many loyal Indian supporters of the British now embraced nationalism. Some nationalists even began asking for complete Home Rule.

Britain was reluctant to give as much as many Indians would have liked, although the government did concede to allowing an Indian assistant to the Secretary of State for India at the Imperial War Cabinet. Britain also granted India's attendance at the Imperial War Conference the same status as that of the Dominions. There were further concerns: in 1917 Russia had collapsed under revolution and trouble grew in Mesopotamia, where Britain had failed to meet its wartime promises of Arab independence. All of this stoked the nationalist movement, causing the British Government to fear serious rebellion in India. Britain thus began to seriously consider eventual self-government for India within the Empire.

In 1918 the Secretary of State for India, Edwin Montague suggested a system of *diarchy*, whereby the British ruled nationally but Indians would control provincial government. This resulted in the Government of India Act 1919, which introduced a national parliament with two houses; it also granted the right to vote to a small percentage of the population and opened up provincial government and some ministerial roles to Indians. However, Indians were still not allowed into senior positions in the Indian Army as had been promised during the war. They were able to rule over segregated Indian units but not over British officers who felt uncomfortable about serving under Indians. The Indian officers, trained at a new Indian version of Sandhurst, believed they were not being treated with the respect they deserved given their wartime sacrifice.

Annie Besant (1847–1933). Interestingly, not all British Indians were against Home Rule. Annie Besant was a British writer and activist for women's rights, secularism and class equality. She became a Theosophist in 1889, following a doctrine of religious philosophy and mysticism. She later moved to India where Theosophy was at its most popular and founded the Central Hindu College at Varansai. As well as being elected president of the Theosophical Society she was one of the first members of the Indian National Congress, later becoming its president. After founding the Indian Home Rule League in 1916 she explained her reasons in *The Case For India* (1917):

India demands Home Rule for two reasons, one essential and vital, the other less important but necessary: firstly, because Freedom is the birthright of every nation; secondly, because her most important interests are now made subservient to the interests of the British Empire without her consent, and her resources are not utilised for her greatest needs.[1]

Besant was arrested for protesting in 1917 but released after a national outcry. One of her friends and fellow Theosophist was Lady Emily Bulwer-Lytton, daughter of the former Viceroy, the 1st Earl of Lytton, and wife of Edwin Lutyens, the architect of New Delhi from 1912–30.

Between the wars

Nationalism and anti-British sentiment grew further still after the Amritsar massacre in 1919 (see pp. 57–58). As judges were shot by women in saris and the Amritsar revenge took a dark turn, a young lawyer and previous supporter of the British Empire, Mohandas (later known as Mahatma, or 'great soul') Gandhi became leader of the newly-formed Indian National Congress party. In 1920 Gandhi began a campaign of non-violent civil disobedience. This campaign, known as *Satyagraha*, resulted in numerous arrests over the next two decades. This resulted in disruption of rail and telegraph systems, and life became less comfortable and more dangerous for many British Indians.

In 1921 the Montague-Chelmsford reforms were implemented, angering both the nationalists and British Conservatives. Within India the reforms took their toll on Anglo-Indians whose jobs were now open to Indians. This affected both Anglo-Indian employment, and their social status. Although some turned to education to help them qualify as teachers and doctors, other Anglo-Indians felt compelled to emigrate to Britain or the Dominions in the hope of receiving better treatment. Nevertheless, life for Anglo-Indians and British still in India had to continue. Memories of everyday life in India in this period can be found in George Roche's *Childhood in India: Tales from Sholapur*.

The Non-Cooperation Movement continued to grow throughout the 1920s and civil disobedience increased, especially in urban areas. As nationalists had not been assuaged by the 1919 Act, the Simon Commission examined the reforms in 1927 but Congress leader Motilal Nehru rejected these and drafted his own constitution. Ramsay Macdonald's Labour Government of 1930 was more sympathetic to nationalism, suggesting further moves towards self-government and releasing Gandhi from prison. This introduced a short period of calm throughout India.

However, the 1931 Conservative-dominated Government failed to continue the reforms, resulting in Gandhi leading a further civil disobedience campaign and being imprisoned. With the 1935 Government of India Act provincial government came under Indian control and the British began to realize that independence was probably inevitable. This appeased the Nationalists to an extent, although they continued to demand fewer unelected members and self-determination for foreign and financial affairs, and the Army.

Second World War

India during the Second World War was largely a military base. Once again Indian volunteers were asked to sacrifice themselves for the British Empire. This support was essential and the government struggled against Congress opposition to Indian involvement. Stafford Cripps, a Labour minister in the wartime British coalition Government and a supporter of Indian nationalism, was compelled to bargain with India, offering Dominion status or secession after the war in return for Indian military involvement. However, the Nationalists refused and the civil disobedience continued.

Politicians in Britain, meanwhile, remained concerned about the logistics of the campaign's demands. On 5 August 1942 Cripps made a prescient Statement on India, saying, 'Gandhi has asked that the British Government should walk out of India and leave the Indian people to settle differences among themselves, even if it means chaos and confusion.' Congress passed the Quit India resolution on 8 August 1942 initiating 'a mass struggle on non-violent lines under the inevitable leadership of Gandhi*ji*'.[2] This led to the imprisonment of both Gandhi and Jawaharlal Nehru, the British-educated statesman who succeeded his father as Congress President in 1929. The British in India suffered as hostility increased; from 1942 Nationalists shouted the new slogan, 'Quit India!' at them, and assassinations of officials and policemen took place.

Another problem for Britain during the war was the extreme nationalist, Subhas Chandra Bose, who became an ally of Germany, Italy and Japan. In summer 1943 Bose received command of the Indian National Army (INA), comprising Indian former PoWs freed by the Japanese. This Army fought against the Allied nations and many of its own countrymen, although the alternative was probably to perish in a PoW camp. Bose created a Free India government based in the Andaman Isles (and Rangoon from 1944) and declared war on the Allies. After losing the battle of Imphal the INA surrendered in May 1945. Despite escaping, Bose died in an aeroplane crash the following August.

151

As violence escalated among some of the nationalists, the police and Army were ordered to retaliate against the rebels. The resulting loss of life shocked many, especially those Muslims who did not share Gandhi's enthusiasm for Quit India.

Not all Britons agreed with the British Government: Madeleine Slade (1892–1982) worked alongside Gandhi (who renamed her Mirabehn), in the struggle for independence and continued to promote his ideals after his death. In 1982 she received the *Padma Vibhushan*, India's second-highest civilian honour, in recognition of her work.

In 1943 the rice crop failed in Bengal. The government, distracted by the capture of Burma, did not act quickly enough and through the summer 11,000 people in Calcutta died of starvation each week. Later millions more Bengalis perished as a result of the unregulated market forces. The enormity of the famine increased the anti-British feeling across India that lasted into peacetime.

By 1946 after several years of war Britain was left shattered and impoverished. Mutinies occurred among Navy personnel in Bombay in 1946. Previously India had been in debt to Britain but now, for the first time, Britain was in debt to those she ruled. This gave the Indian Nationalists real power. Many Britons wanted to leave, particularly as resentment of the British regime was reaching new heights. However, there was concern over how peacefully this could be achieved. The Nationalists were divided in their aims; the Hindu Congress demanded a united India; the Muslim League insisted on a separate Muslim state.

Partition and the Transfer of Power

As early as 1939, both Britons and Indians were coming to realize that future partition was likely. Mohammad Ali Jinnah, leader of the Muslim League, had already decided on a name for the new Muslim state. Student Choudray Rahmat Ali had written a pamphlet in 1933 entitled 'Now or Never: Are we to live or perish forever?' in which he created 'Pakstan' as an acronym from the first letter of the states which would form the new land: Punjab, Afghania (the North-West Territories), Kashmir and Sind. Tan was short for Baluchistan. The future country soon became known as Pakistan.

Many Britons in India were fiercely against partition, particularly of the Indian Army into Hindu and Muslim armies, because of their pride in the unified India created by Britain. Gandhi was also strongly against partition, saying in 1946, 'Before partitioning India, my body will have to be cut into two pieces.'

However, the Muslim League did not want a minority Muslim presence in a Hindu-dominated government. There were fears that centuries-old resentments would reappear resulting in anti-Muslim discrimination. In 1946 Viceroy Lord Wavell suggested 'an interim government of six Congress Hindus (including one untouchable), five Muslim Leaguers, a Sikh, a Parsi and an Indian Christian'.[3] Jinnah was happy with the plan, and it was believed Nehru was too but Gandhi encouraged Congress to reject it, as he wanted Muslims within Congress in government rather than as part of a separate Muslim League. Congress rejected the plan but Nehru agreed to the premiership. Jinnah therefore rejected the plan also and never trusted Gandhi again. He announced a Direct Action Day on 16 August. The tensions simmering between the politicians spread among the population and exploded into the Great Calcutta Killing of 1946, with thousands dying in the horrific scenes of violence that emerged. Original material on these events, such as letters from Lord Wavell and minutes from meetings can be found in IOR series L/PJ, or see Earl Archibald Wavell's *The Viceroy's Journal*.

In December Jinnah and Nehru met with members of the British Government to try to come to an agreement. Little progress was made but Wavell's closeness to Congress was making him unpopular with Jinnah and others. Later that month he was replaced by Lord Louis Mountbatten. It was Mountbatten who insisted on a definite date for the transfer of power. Wavell had been working towards a rough date of 31 March 1948 but, under pressure, Attlee presented Mountbatten with a firm date of 1 June 1948. However, tired of the constant disagreements between all parties, Mountbatten announced to a meeting on 3 June 1947 of the Muslim League, Congress and Sikhs in which 'none should be allowed to speak',[4] that the deadline had been changed to 15 August 1947 – just ten weeks away.

Everyone then rushed to finalize arrangements. An Indo-Pakistan Boundary Commission was created, chaired by Sir Cyril Radcliffe, to decide on precise boundaries for the new states and their combined populations of around 400 million socially and culturally diverse people. India was to be divided into a large Hindu state in the centre (India) with a geographically divided Muslim state (Pakistan); one part in the east, the other in the west. Both states would remain in the Commonwealth. The demands of Sikhs for their own national state (Khalistan) in the Punjab and the anti-Muslim sentiments among many were not taken into account. In the end, half of the Punjab was placed in Muslim Pakistan. Despite his protests Radcliffe was given just six weeks to draw the lines on the map that would end Britain's unified India and lead to the homelessness and deaths of millions. Fighting over Kashmir continues into the twenty-first century.

History has judged the British Government's handling of partition harshly; American Indologist Stanley Wolpert called it a *Shameful Flight*. Much of the blame has been laid with Mountbatten, Viceroy from March 1947, who led the rushed negotiations and insisted on an early deadline. The Independence movement which had begun after the First World War finally resulted in India and Pakistan becoming independent at the stroke of midnight on 14 August 1947. Over 400 years of British involvement and nearly 300 years of imperial rule ended with just one tick of a clock.

This is seen as regrettable today in the light of the terrible and violent events that followed that stroke of midnight. Jubilant celebration at being free of Britain turned into chaos. More than 10 million Hindus, Muslims and Sikhs were displaced as they struggled to cross new borders between the now-separate countries of India and Pakistan. More than half a million people were killed in the massacres of the Punjab.

In all more than a million people died. The speed with which partition occurred prevented Indians from moving to areas of safety. Gandhi was horrified by events, begging the combatants to stop, and proceeding to fast. In September 1947 riots in Calcutta ended but on 30 January 1948 Mahatma Gandhi was assassinated by a fellow Hindu, Nathuram Godse, who believed Gandhi had betrayed the Hindu cause.

No-one who lived through these scenes ever forgot them and there are many written testimonies from surviving Indians and Britons. British accounts can be found in *Plain Tales From The Raj*, and *Freedom at Midnight* by Larry Collins and Dominique Lapierre.

Partition was also a difficult time for the Anglo-Indian community: 'The Curious Exclusion of Anglo-Indians from Mass Slaughter during the Partition of India' based on original interviews can be read online at http://home.alphalink.com.au/~agilbert/curious.html.

Political Constitutional Papers on the transfer of power 1942–55 can be found in series L/PO and R/3/1. The 12-volumed work *The Transfer of Power 1942–47* edited by Nicholas Mansergh et al is on the open-access shelves in AAS.

Pakistan & Bangladesh; Sri Lanka

The term 'South Asia' now includes India, Pakistan, Bangladesh and Sri Lanka.

Ceylon became independent on 4 February 1948, and was renamed as the Republic of Sri Lanka within the Commonwealth on 22 May 1971.

India became a republic in 1950 but remained a member of the Commonwealth and retained a prime ministerial form of government.

East Pakistan became the separate state of Bangladesh in 1971.

The Departure of the British from India

In the hurry to meet Mountbatten's deadline, little consideration had been given to the thousands of British and Anglo-Indians for whom India was home. Passenger lists (see Chapter 6) from this date show many Britons travelling from India to British ports, some for the first time in their lives. Britons were offered free passage in return for registering with the authorities and received letters of authority and ration books. Although most Britons and Anglo-Indians referred to Britain as 'Home' with a capital H, many had had family roots in India for centuries. Not surprisingly, a number of Europeans were reluctant to leave.

The situation was particularly difficult for the Anglo-Indians who had to choose where to live. Were they more English or more Indian? Some Anglo-Indians did not even know of Indian ancestry but with Italian, Portuguese or other non-British European ancestry or dark skin, they would be classed as Anglo-Indian. Many chose to go to the relatively new countries of the Dominions where they felt they could prosper. Australia's climate also appealed. However, young Anglo-Indians tended to find life in Britain easier than their elders, for whom the cold climate and occasional racism was difficult. Today Anglo-Indians live all over the world in countries such as the UK, Australia, New Zealand, the USA Canada, Dubai, and, of course, India, Pakistan and Bangladesh. More Anglo-Indians live in Kolkata than anywhere else in India. Lord Linlithgow said of the Anglo-Indians: 'The Community has made a contribution of a real and permanent nature to India: it has produced many figures of outstanding capacity in the past and the work done by its members has been of real, lasting value.'

English people were not always very welcoming to the British Indians in the 1940s and 50s. However, former members of the forces who had served in India in the war were often pleased to meet others who had lived there; Noel Gunther found himself welcomed by ex-forces workers at Southern Railways when he began work with them in the 1960s. The cultural differences were also not always too much of a shock: Anglo-Indians were familiar with British food, for example. Noel Gunther's Dutch-British family in Calcutta ate curry only once a week among a diet of stews, casseroles and pot roasts. Others continued with an Indian diet in their own homes, cooking curries which visiting family members would take home in tiffin tins, eating a daily breakfast of kedgeree, or buying spices from the increasing numbers of shops that sold them in late twentieth-century Britain. And, for those Europeans who chose to remain in India, the tradition of tea at four o'clock continued as before.

The Stayers-On: Records of the British in India from 1948

After independence, Britons tended to be held in less respect by Indians and some found themselves in a lower social class than during the British Indian period. In 1951, 'the Managing Director of Andrew Yule [a managing agency], Sir Leslie Cameron, was killed by a mob of Hindus while trying to protect a Muslim who was sharing his car at the time'.[5]

According to the British High Commission in India in the early 1970s:

> In 1947, about 55,000 British civilians returned home so that, in 1951, there were 28,000 British residents in India, most of whom had been born in the United Kingdom. By 1961 the number had halved to around 14,000, and ten years later it had more than halved again to 6,500.[6]

The stayers-on are those who remained in Empire countries after they became independent. Many did not want to return to Britain under a Labour government. In India, life continued as it always had for many of the stayers-on, right into the mid-sixties: 'in 1964 there was still a thriving British commercial community in Calcutta and British planters still dominated the tea gardens.'[7] The Gunther family (pictured) remained in India until the 1960s. Records are sparser in the British Library after this date but are worth checking. Useful secondary sources for finding family members are the *Indo-British Review* – a magazine that covered India 1932–94 – and *Chowkidar*, the magazine of BACSA (see p. 111). Social clubs, such as the Tollygunge Club (www.thetollygungeclub.com) in southern Kolkata, remained enclaves of the British until 1969 when the first Indian President was elected, and retains records of British members. The club still operates in traditional ways, and there are numerous British surnames among the committee members, such as a Mrs Gitanjali Jolly.

However, in the mid 1960s two events occurred which changed life irrevocably for the British and Anglo-Indians. In 1966 the Colonial Office merged with the Commonwealth Relations Office (previously the

Dominions Office). Far worse was the fateful day of 6 June 1966 – 6/6/66 as it became known – when the rupee was devalued and the cost of exchange to pounds sterling increased by over a third. These events affected the business community (mostly based around Calcutta) so badly that many decided they could remain in India no longer.

Despite this there were some who stayed until the 1980s, often until they died. Those who stayed were known as *Koi hais* or the women as *mems* (short for *memsahibs*). More details, including memories of life in India, obituaries, reunions and a page for finding lost relatives or old friends such as those who worked in North-East India in the tea industry, on ferries etc can be found at the website www.koi-hai.com.

Tracing Relatives who have left India

There are numerous resources for tracing people in Britain, including social networking sites, electoral registers and telephone directories. One method for finding relatives is to trace down the family tree using death certificates and probate records, as well as other genealogical sources. Useful websites for this search include the social networking pages mentioned in Chapter 1.

Australia. There were links between India and Australia from as early as the eighteenth century, and a number of orphans were sent there in the nineteenth century. Many British Indians in the twentieth century were keen to travel to Australia and other dominions as – unlike in India – they could buy land there. More information on these connections can be found at the FIBIS website http://wiki.fibis.org/index.php?title= Australia. There is a very active branch of FIBIS in Australia, led by the Australia Membership Liaison.

One of the most useful websites for finding family members in Australia is Trove, from the National Library of Australia http://trove. nla.gov.au, which contains millions of records. For introductions to Australian genealogical research and indexes to passenger arrivals from India, see the guides at the National Archives of Australia www.naa. gov.au. The record offices and libraries of individual states are also worth checking, particularly that of South Australia http://www.slsa. sa.gov.au/manning/sa/immigra/misc.htm.

New Zealand. New Zealand was also a popular destination for Anglo-Indians as it offered employment and land. The National Library of New Zealand has a family history research guide at http://www.natlib.

govt.nz/services/get-advice/family-history. You can find a searchable database of fifty-eight newspaper titles at Papers Past http://papers past.natlib.govt.nz/cgi-bi/paperspast.

India. For civil registration records, you will need to contact the individual state where the event was registered. For more details, see the Indian Government's website http://india.gov.in/howdo/howdoi. php?service=2. Obtaining copies of death certificates in India can be difficult but some may be ordered online (such as those of Chennai). Probate records can be obtained through the sub-registrar's office of the relevant *taluk* (municipal area). Otherwise, you may find your relatives through people-finding websites based in India, like www.jantakhoj. com or social networking sites, like Twitter and Facebook.

Legacy

At the end of British involvement, the Indian subcontinent was completely different from the India encountered by the EIC merchants in 1601. The legacy of British Indian ancestors is clearly rich and varied.

Some look back on Britain's involvement in India as troubled with political controversy, social segregation and military conflict. However, others point to its achievements. Hugh Purcell summarizes the legacy well, providing a list of entities created under British India or which exist as a result of British influence there. These include:

- the railways
- the political constitution and civil service
- the judiciary
- canals
- the managing agency commercial system
- the regimental traditions of the Indian Army
- the roads laid in previously unreachable places by marching armies
- cricket
- the English (and Anglo-Indian) language
- the Christian churches
- the tea industry
- British architecture
- private education
- the heritage industry.

There are also tiger conservation projects with maharajahs, like the Tiger Tops Jungle Lodge in Chitwan National Park, Nepal, which developed out of the British tiger hunts. For further tiger projects, see www.tiger awareness.co.uk.

The legacy of your individual ancestor is now yours to discover. It is hoped that you will be able to do this successfully by using the many genealogical and historical resources that are detailed within this book.

Notes

1. Annie Besant, *The Case for India*, 1917.
2. Nehru, *The Discovery of India*, p. 454.
3. Alex von Tunzelmann, *Indian Summer*, p. 142 (2007).
4. Ibid., p. 199.
5. Hugh Purcell, *After the Raj: The Last Stayers-On and the Legacy of British India*, (2008).
6. Ibid.
7. Ibid., preface.

GOVERNORS & VICEROYS OF INDIA*

Governors-General of India (1773–1858)

1773–1785 Warren Hastings (1732–1818)

1785–1786 Sir John Macpherson, 1st Baronet (*c*1745–1821)

1786–1793 Charles Cornwallis, 1st Marquess of Cornwallis (1738–1805)

1793–1798 Sir John Shore, 1st Baronet (1751–1834)

1798 (March–May) Sir Alured Clarke (1744–1832); acting Governor-General

1798–1805 Richard Wellesley, 2nd Earl of Mornington (1760–1842)

1805 (July–Oct) Charles Cornwallis, 1st Marquess of Cornwallis (1738–1805)

1805–1807 Sir George Hilario Barlow, 1st Baronet (1763–1846)

1807–1813 Gilbert Elliot-Murray-Kynynmound, 1st Earl of Minto (1751–1814)

1813–1823 Francis Rawdon Hastings, 1st Marquess of Hastings and 2nd Earl of Moira (1754–1826)

1823 (Jan–Aug) John Adam (1779–1825); acting Governor-General

1823–1828 William Pitt Amherst,1st Earl Amherst of Arracan (1773–1857)

1828 (March–July) (William) Butterworth Bayley (1781–1860); acting Governor-General

1828–1835 Lord William Henry Cavendish-Bentinck [known as Lord William Bentinck] (1774–1839)

* From Oxford Dictionary of National Biography (ODNB).

1835–1836 Sir Charles Theophilus Metcalfe (1785–1846); acting Governor-General

1836–1842 George Eden, Earl of Auckland (1784–1849)

1842–1844 Edward Law, 2nd Baron Ellenborough (1790–1871)

1844 (June–July) William Wilberforce Bird (d.1857); acting Governor-General

1844–1848 Henry Hardinge, 1st Viscount Hardinge of Lahore (1785–1856)

1848–1856 James Andrew Broun Ramsay, 1st Marquess of Dalhousie (1812–1860)

1856–1858 Charles John Canning, Viscount Canning (1812–1862)

Viceroys of India (1858–1947)

1858–1862 Charles John Canning, Earl Canning (1812–1862)

1862–1863 James Bruce, 8th Earl of Elgin and 12th Earl of Kincardine (1811–1863)

1863 (Nov–Dec) Sir Robert Cornelis Napier (1810–1890); acting Viceroy

1863–1864 Sir William Thomas Denison (1804–1871); acting Viceroy

1864–1869 Sir John Laird Mair Lawrence, 1st Baronet (1811–1879)

1869–1872 Richard Southwell Bourke, 6th Earl of Mayo (1822–1872)

1872 (Feb) Sir John Strachey (1823–1907); acting Viceroy

1872 (Feb–May) Francis Napier, 1st Baron Ettrick (1819–1898); acting Viceroy

1872–1876 Thomas George Baring, 2nd Baron Northbrook (1826–1904)

1876–1880 Edward Robert Bulwer-Lytton, 2nd Baron Lytton (1831–1891)

1880–1884 George Frederick Samuel Robinson, 1st Marquess of Ripon (1827–1909)

1884–1888 Frederick Temple Hamilton-Temple-Blackwood, 1st Earl of Dufferin and Viscount Clandeboye (1826–1902)

1888–1894 Henry Charles Keith Petty-Fitzmaurice, 5th Marquess of Lansdowne (1845–1927)

1894–1899 Victor Alexander Bruce, 9th Earl of Elgin and 13th Earl of Kincardine (1849–1917)

1899–1905 George Nathaniel Curzon, Baron Curzon of Kedleston (1859–1925)

1905–1910 Gilbert John Elliot-Murray-Kynynmound, 4th Earl of Minto (1845–1914)

1910–1916 Charles Hardinge, 1st Baron Hardinge of Penshurst (1858–1944)

1916–1921 Frederic John Napier Thesiger, 3rd Baron Chelmsford (1868–1933)

1921–1926 Rufus Daniel Isaacs, 1st Earl of Reading (1860–1935)

1925 (April–Aug) Victor Alexander George Robert Bulwer-Lytton, 2nd Earl of Lytton (1876–1947); acting Viceroy

1926–1931 Edward Frederick Lindley Wood, Baron Irwin (1881–1959)

1929 (June–Nov) George Joachim Goschen, 2nd Viscount Goschen (1866–1952); acting Viceroy

1931–1936 Freeman Freeman-Thomas, 1st Earl of Willingdon (1866–1941)

1936–1943 Victor Alexander John Hope, 2nd Marquess of Linlithgow (1887–1952)

1943–1947 Archibald Percival Wavell, Viscount Wavell (1883–1950)

1947 (Feb–Aug) Louis Francis Albert Victor Nicholas Mountbatten, 1st Viscount Mountbatten of Burma (1900–1979)

BIBLIOGRAPHY

History of British India

Bayly, Chris, *Empire and Information: Information Gathering and Social Communication in India 1780–1870* (Cambridge: Cambridge University Press, 1996)

Brown, J.M., 'India' in Brown, J.M. and W.R. Louis, *The Oxford History of the British Empire vol. 4 The Twentieth Century* (Oxford: Oxford University Press, 1999)

Ferguson, Niall, *Empire* (London: Penguin, 2004)

Kincaid, Dennis, *British Social life in India, 1608–1937* (London: Routledge & Kegan Paul, 1974)

Marshall, P.J., 'Bengal: The British Bridgehead, Eastern India, 1740–1828', *The New Cambridge History of India*, vol. 2 (Cambridge: Cambridge University Press, 1987)

Phillips, Kevin P., *Wealth and Democracy* (London: Broadway Books, 2003)

Porter, Bernard, *The Lion's Share: A Short History of British Imperialism 1850–2004* (Harlow: Pearson, 2004)

Sears, Stephen W., *The Horizon History of the British Empire* (New York: American Heritage Publishing, in association with BBC/Time-Life, 1973)

Memoir

Quick, Diana, *A Tug on A Thread* (London: Virago, 2009)

Wilkinson, Theon, *Two Monsoons* (London: Duckworth, 1976)

East India Company

Allen's Indian mail, and register of intelligence for British and foreign India, China, and all parts of the East (London: Allen & Co., vol. 9, 1851)

The Oriental annual, or, Scenes in India (London: E. Bull, 1834)

Dalrymple, William, *White Mughals* (London: Harper Perennial, 2004)

Daniell, William, Hobart Caunter and Thomas Bacon, *The Oriental annual, or, Scenes in India* (London: E. Bull, 1834)
Farrington, Anthony, *The Records of the East India College Haileybury and Other Institutions* (London: British Library, 1976)
Fay, Eliza, *Letters* (London: Hogarth Press, 1925)
Keay, John, *The Honourable Company: A History of the English East India Company* (London: HarperCollins, 1993)
Lawson, Philip, *The East India Company: A History* (London: Longman, 1993)
Maitland, Julia, *Letters from Madras, During the Years 1836–1839* (London: J. Murray, 1846)
Morgan, Richard, *FIBIS Fact File: No. 3 Indian Directories* (London: Families In British India Society, 2009)
Pickett, Catherine, *Bibliography of the East India Company: Books, Pamphlets and Other Materials Printed Between 1600 and 1785* (London: British Library Publishing, 2011)
Spear, Percival, *The Nabobs: A Study of the Life of the English in Eighteenth-Century India* (Oxford: Oxford University Press, 1932)

Robert Clive and the Battle of Plassey

Ali, Ruhana; Imran Jamal et al., *Plassey's Legacy: Young Londoners Explore the Hidden Story of the East India Company* (London: Brick Lane Circle, 2010)
Harvey, Robert, *Clive: The Life and Death of a British Emperor* (London: Sceptre, 1999)
Holwell, John Zephaniah, *A Genuine Narrative of the Deplorable Deaths of the English Gentlemen and others who were suffocated in the Black Hole* (London: Millar, 1758)
Little, J.H., 'The Black Hole – The Question of Holwell's Veracity' in *Bengal Past & Present* (Calcutta: Calcutta Historical Society, 1915)

Family History Research

Asiatic Journal (London: Allen & Co.,1816–45)
Bengal Past and Present (Calcutta: Calcutta Historical Society, 1907-)
India Office Records: Guide to Wills – Probate, Administrations and Inventories, with extracts from list of accountant-general's records [IOR Lists 203a] (London: British Library)

Baxter, I.A., *Baxter's Guide: Biographical Sources in the India Office Records* (Gateshead: FIBIS & The British Library, 3rd Edition, 2004)

——, *India Office Records: a brief guide to sources* (London: British Library, 4th Edition, 2004)

Bevan, Amanda, *Tracing Your Ancestors in The National Archives* (London: PRO Publications, 2006)

Charles, Geraldine, 'Anglo-Indian Ancestry' in *Genealogists' Magazine* vol. 27, no. 3 (London: SOG, 2001)

Drennan, Basil St G. (ed.), *The Keble College Centenary Register* (Oxford: Keble College, 1970)

Farrington, Anthony, *Guide to the records of the India Office Military Department: IOR/L/MIL & L/WS* (London: India Office Library and Records/Foreign and Commonwealth Office, 1981)

Malden, C.H. (ed.), *List of burials at Madras from 1660 to 1746, compiled from the register of St Mary's Church, Fort St George* (Madras: Government Press, 1903)

Moir, Martin, *A General Guide to the India Office Records* (London: British Library, 1988)

Naipaul, V.S., *India: A Million Mutinies* (London: Vintage, 1998)

Phillimore, R.H., *Historical records of the Survey of India* (Dehra Dun: Survey of India, 1945–48)

Rhé-Irving, Miles & Philipe, George William De, *Inscriptions on Christian tombs or monuments, Volumes 1 & 2* (Lahore: Government Press, 1912; reprinted as *Soldiers of the Raj*, Uckfield: Naval & Military Press, 2002)

Taylor, N.C., *Sources for Anglo-Indian Genealogy in the Library of the Society of Genealogists* (London: SOG, 1990)

Yeo, G., (compiler), *The British Overseas* (London: Guildhall Library, 3rd Edition, 1995)

Military

Indian Army List (Calcutta etc: Defence Department, 1889–1947)

Dunlop, E. E., *The War Diaries of "Weary" Dunlop: Java and the Burma-Thailand Railway, 1942–45* (Ringwood, Victoria: Penguin, 1990)

Bailey, Peter, *Researching Ancestors in the East India Company's Armies* (London: FIBIS, 2006)

Chalker, Jack, *Burma Railway: Original War Drawings of POW Jack Chalker* (Somerset: Mercer Books, 2007)

Crawford, D.G., *Roll of the Indian Medical Service 1615–1930* (London: Thacker, 1930)

Crowder, Norman K., *British Army Pensioners Abroad, 1712–1899* (Baltimore: Clearfield Company, 1995)

David, Saul, *The Indian Mutiny: 1857* (London: Penguin, 2003)

Dodwell & Miles, *List of officers of the Indian Army from 1760 to 1834* (London: Longman, Orme, Brown & Co., 1838)

Gimlette, Lieutenant Colonel G.H.D., *A Postscript to the Records of the Indian Mutiny: An attempt to trace the subsequent careers and fate of the rebel Bengal regiments, 1857–1858* (London: Witherby, 1927)

Guy, Alan J. & Peter B. Boyden, *Soldiers of the Raj, The Indian Army 1600–1947* (London: National Army Museum Chelsea, 1997)

Hibbert, Christopher, *The Great Mutiny* (London: Allen Lane, 1978)

Hodson, V.C.P., *List of the Officers of the Bengal Army, 1758–1834*, 4 vols (London, Constable, 1927–1947)

Mason, Philip, *A Matter of Honour: An account of the Indian Army its officers and men* (London: Cape, 1974)

Omissi, David, *The Sepoy and the Raj: The Indian Army, 1860–1940* (London: Macmillan, 1994)

Seton, R.E., *The Indian Mutiny 1857–58: A Guide to Source Material in the India Office Library and Records* (London: British Library, 1986)

Sleeman, William, *Rambles and Recollections of an Indian Official* (Project Gutenberg Ebook, 2005)

Visram, Rosina, 'The First World War and the Indian Soldiers' in *Indo-British Review, A Journal of History* (Madras: Indo-British Historical Society, vol. xvi, No. 2, June 1989)

Visram, Rosina, *Ayahs, Lascars and Princes: Indians in Britain 1700–1947* (London: Pluto Press, 1986)

Railways

Awasthi, Aruna, *History and Development of Railways in India* (New Delhi: Deep and Deep Publications, 1994)

Bell, S. Peter, *A biographical index of British engineers in the 19th Century* (New York: Garland, 1975)

Davidson, Edward, *The railways of India: with an account of their rise, progress, and construction* (London: E. & F.N. Spon, 1868)

Davis, Clarence B. and Kenneth E. Wilburn Jr. with Ronald E. Robinson (eds), *Railway Imperialism* (New York: Greenwood Press, 1991)

Ghosh, S., *Railways in India – A Legend* (Kolkata: Jogemaya Prokashani, 2002)

Kerr, I., *Building the Railways of the Raj* (Delhi: Oxford University Press, 1995)

Khosla, G.S.A., *History of Indian Railways* (India: Ministry of Railways, 1988)

Kipling, Rudyard, 'Among the Railway Folk' in *From Sea to Sea: Letters of Travel* (New York: Doubleday and McClure Company, 1899)

Mukherjee, Hena, *The Early History of The East India Railway 1845–1879* (FIRMA KLM Private Ltd.: Calcutta, 1994)

Otte, T.G., and Keith Neilson (eds), *Railways and International Politics: Paths of Empire, 1848–1945* (New York: Routledge, 2006)

Richards, Tom, *Was your Grandfather a Railwayman?* (Bristol: FFHS, 2002)

Satow, M. and R. Desmond, *Railways of the Raj* (London: Scolar Press, 1980)

Sharp, *Obituaries of British Engineers 1901–1920* (London: Science Museum, 1993)

Tully, Mark, *India's Unending Journey* (London: Rider, 2008)

Wilding, Hugh, FRSA, *FIBIS Fact File: No. 4 Research sources for Indian Railways, 1845–1947* (London: FIBIS, 2009)

Anglo-Indians

List of East India Company's Civil and and Military Servants (*Bengal Asylum Press Almanac*, August 1875)

Anthony, Frank, *Britain's Betrayal in India: The Story of the Anglo Indian Community* (London: Simon Wallenberg Press, 2007)

Cocker, Max, *Lovedale: The Lawrence Memorial Royal Military School, South India: a personal account* (Glasgow: M. E. Cocker, 1988)

Hawes, Christopher J., *Poor relations: The Making of a Eurasian Community in British India 1773–1833* (London: Routledge, 1996)

Lushington, Charles, *The History, Design and Present State of the Religious, Benevolent and Charitable Institutions Founded by The British in Calcutta* (Calcutta: BMOS, 1824)

Shephard, Ethel, *A Marooned People; the Anglo-Indian community* (London: S.P.G., 1930)

The *Raj*

Englishwoman in India: information for ladies on their outfit, furniture [&c.] by a lady resident (1864 accessed via http://books.google.co.uk)

Indian Mutiny Medal Roll 1857–1859 (British Forces, 1998)

Allen, Charles (ed.), *Plain Tales from the Raj* (London: Andre Deutsch, 1975)

Baxter, *Biographical Sources in the India Office Records* 3rd Edition (2004)

Brendon, V., *Children of the Raj* (London: Weidenfeld & Nicolson, 2005)

Chaudhuri, Nupur, 'Memsahib and Motherhood in Nineteenth-Century India', in *Victorian Studies 31*, no. 4: 517–535 (Bloomington: Indiana University Press, 1988)

Diver, Maud, *The Englishwoman in India* (Edinburgh: W. Blackwood & Sons, 1909)

Fayrer, J., *European Child-Life in India*, OIOC Tract 820 (London: J.A. Churchill, 1873)

Fowler, Marion, *Below the Peacock Fan* (Markham, Ontario: Viking, 1987)

Gabb, A., *The Anglo-Indian Legacy 1600–1947: A Brief Guide to British Raj India History* (Rev. 2nd Edition, Overton: The author, 2003)

Ghosh, Durba, *Sex and the Family in Colonial India: The Making of Empire* (Cambridge: Cambridge University Press, 2006)

Kipling, Rudyard, *Something of myself and other autobiographical writings* (Cambridge: Cambridge University Press, 1935)

——, 'The Light That Failed' in *The Works of Rudyard Kipling* (accessed via http://www.gutenberg.org/ebooks/2334)

Wolpert, Stanley, *A New History of India* (Oxford: Oxford University Press, 1977)

Nationalism, Independence and Afterwards

Barker, A.J., *The Neglected War: Mesopotamia 1914–1918* (London: Faber & Faber, 1967)

Collins, Larry and Dominique Lapierre, *Freedom at Midnight* (London: HarperCollins, 1997)

Foss, Michael, *Out of India* (London: Michael O'Mara, 2002)

Galbraith, J.K., *A Life in Our Times* (Boston: Houghton Mifflin, 1981)

Mansergh, Nicholas et al (eds), *The Transfer of Power 1942–47* (London: HMSO, 1970–83)

Moore, R.J., *Escape from Empire: the Attlee Government and the Indian Problem* (Oxford: Clarendon, 1983)

Moorhouse, Geoffrey, *India Britannica* (London: Harvill Press, 1983)

Nehru, *The Discovery of India*(Oxford: OUP India, 1989)

Pettinger, Tejvan, *Biography of Annie Besant* (Oxford: www.biography online.net, 2011)

Purcell, Hugh, *After the Raj: the last stayers-on and the legacy of British India* (Stroud: The History Press, 2008)

Roberts, Andrew, *Eminent Churchillians* (London: Phoenix, 1995)

Roche, George, *Childhood in India: Tales from Sholapur* (London: Radcliffe, 1994)

Tunzelmann, Alex Von, *Indian Summer* (London: Simon & Schuster, 2007)

Wavell, Earl Archibald, Penderel Moon (ed.), *The Viceroy's Journal* (Oxford: Oxford University Press, 1973)

Probate

India Office Records: Guide to Wills – Probate, Administrations and Inventories, with extracts from list of accountant-general's records [IOR Lists 203a]

Clare, Wallace, *Irish Genealogical Guides: a Guide to Copies & Abstracts of Irish Wills (First Series), Volume 1* (March, Cambridgeshire: Sharman & Co., 1930)

Grannum, Karen and Nigel Taylor, *Wills and Probate Records*, 2nd Edition (London: The National Archives, 2009)

Jolly, Emma, 'Open Access Microfilms in the Asia, Pacific & Africa Collections of the British Library' in *Genealogists' Magazine* (London: SOG, September 2008)

Maritime

Beattie, M.H., *On the Hooghly* (London: Philip Allan, 1935)

Coates, W.H., *The Old Country Trade of the East Indies* (London: Imray, Laurie, Norie & Wilson, 1911 accessed via www.archive.org)

Colledge, J.J. & Ben Warlow, *Ships of the Royal Navy – The Complete Record of all Fighting Ships of the Royal Navy from the 15th Century to the Present* (London: Chatham Publishing, 2006 revised)

Eibl-Kaye, Dr Geoffrey, 'Indian Ship Letters 1814–1819' (London: Royal Philatelic Society, 2004 http://www.rpsl.org.uk/indian_ship_letters/index.html)

Farrington, Anthony, *A Biographical Index of the East India Maritime Service Officers 1600–1834* (London: British Library, 1999)

——, *Shipping and Ship-Building in India 1736–1839* (London: India Office Record, 1995)

Fuller, Tony, *Memorial Inscriptions at the East India Company Chapel, Poplar* (Hornchurch: Armenians in India Press, 1998)

Hardy, Horatio Charles, *Register of Ships of the East India Company* (London: Black, Parry and Kingsbury, 1811)

Howarth, David & Stephen, *The Story of P&O: Peninsular and Oriental Steam Navigation Company* (London: Weidenfeld and Nicolson, 1994)

Labey & Brice, *The History Of The Bengal Pilot Service* (Document at the National Maritime Museum, Ref. THS/12/1–9, 1963)

Lambert, Andrew, 'Strategy, Policy and Shipbuilding: the Bombay Dockyard, the Indian Navy and Imperial Security in Eastern Seas, 1784–1869' in H.V. Bowen, Margarette Lincoln & Nigel Rigby (eds), *The Worlds of the East India Company* (London & Leicester: The Boydell Press, NMM & University of Leicester, 2002)

Northcote Parkinson, C., (ed.), *The Trade Winds* (London: George Allen & Unwin Ltd., 1948)

Pappalardo, Bruno, *Tracing Your Naval Ancestors* (London: The National Archives, 2003)

Smith, K., C.T. & M.J. Watts, *Records of Merchant Shipping and Seamen* (London: PRO Publications, 1998)

Anglo-Indian Glossary

Hankin, Nigel, *Hanklyn-Janklin* (New Delhi: India Research Press, 2003)

Tea

Merchants' magazine and commercial review (New York: F. Hunt, 1840)

Barker, George, *A Tea Planter's Life in Assam* (Calcutta: Thacker, Spink & Co., 1884)

Boswell, James, *The life of Samuel Johnson, LL.D., including a Journal of his tour to the Hebrides, Vol 9* (London: J. Murray, 1835)

Moxham, Roy, *A Brief History of Tea: Addiction, Exploitation and Empire* (London: Robinson, 2009)

Taylor's *Maps of the following Tea Districts: Darjeeling, Terai, Jalpaiguri and Dooars, Darrang, Golaghat, Jorhat Nowgong, Sibsagar, Lakhimpur, Dibrugarh, Cachar, Sylhet, with complete Index to all Tea Gardens* (Calcutta: Thacker, Spink & Co., 1910)

INDEX